...stablished
...vel brands,
...s in travel.

...years our
...he secrets
...he world,
...a wealth of
experience and a passion for travel.

**Rely on Thomas Cook as your
travelling companion on your next trip
and benefit from our unique heritage.**

Thomas Cook **pocket** guides

BUCHAREST

Thomas Cook

Thomas
Cook

Your travelling companion since 1873

Written by Craig Turp, updated by Debbie Stowe

Published by Thomas Cook Publishing
A division of Thomas Cook Tour Operations Limited
Company registration no. 3772199 England
The Thomas Cook Business Park, 9 Coningsby Road,
Peterborough PE3 8SB, United Kingdom
Email: books@thomascook.com, Tel: +44 (0) 1733 416477
www.thomascookpublishing.com

Produced by Cambridge Publishing Management Ltd
Burr Elm Court, Main Street, Caldecote CB23 7NU
www.cambridgepm.co.uk

ISBN: 978-1-84848-405-4

© 2007, 2009 Thomas Cook Publishing
This third edition © 2011 Thomas Cook Publishing
Text © Thomas Cook Publishing
Maps © Thomas Cook Publishing/PCGraphics (UK) Limited
Transport map © Communicarta Limited

Series Editor: Karen Beaulah
Production/DTP: Steven Collins

Printed and bound in Spain by GraphyCems

Cover photography © Lonely Planet/SuperStock

CONTENTS

SYMBOLS KEY

The following symbols are used throughout this book:

ⓐ address ☏ telephone ⓦ website address ⓔ email address
🕒 opening times ⓝ public transport connections ❶ important

The following symbols are used on the maps:

🛫	airport	▪	point of interest
➕	hospital	○	city
🛡	police station	○	large town
🚌	bus station	○	small town
🚆	railway station	═	motorway
Ⓜ	metro	—	main road
❶	numbers denote featured		minor road
	cafés & restaurants	—	railway

Hotels and restaurants are graded by approximate price as follows:
£ budget price **££** mid-range price **£££** expensive

Abbreviations & translations used in addresses:

Al	Aleaa (Alley or Mews)	Calea means Avenue
B-dul	Bulevardul (Boulevard)	Piața means Square
Șos	Șoseaua (Boulevard)	
Str	Strada (Street)	

❿ *The magnificent courthouse is reflected on the Dâmbovița River*

 **INTRODUCING**
Bucharest

Introduction

Hot and dusty, Bucharest in high summer is more North Africa than Europe; freezing and usually covered with snow for months at a time, in midwinter it's more like the Arctic. Chaos reigns all year round – regardless of the weather – and the dynamism of a city playing catch-up with the rest of the continent can often make the place bewildering; therein lies the charm.

Even its fiercest advocate would readily admit that when taken at face value Bucharest is not Europe's most appealing capital. Very little of the old Bucharest – dubbed Little Paris in the 1920s and 1930s by the procession of famous travellers who came here – remains: the vast majority of the city's buildings date from the communist period, when the need to build hundreds of thousands of apartments at great speed meant aesthetics lost out. Within the socialist realism, however, gems remain: the art deco blocks of Bulevardul Magheru, the neoclassical University and the crumbling secessionist houses of Lipscani – the one part of the Old Town that survived central planning.

But most people visit Bucharest for its energy, rather than its sights. The place simply buzzes with young and dynamic people from all over Romania; the country's brightest and best all come here to study, and most decide to stay for good. You'll see evidence of Bucharest's dynamism everywhere, from the construction boom of the early 2000s that saw shiny new skyscrapers appear from nowhere – even if the economic crisis has called a temporary halt – to the trendy nightspots that are attracting the finest DJs in the world.

As life-affirming destinations go, Bucharest is as good as it gets right now, and a weekend is enough to see the few real sights there are. If you do have more time, the palaces that surround the capital make tranquil kickback destinations, while just an hour or so on Romania's new fast trains will deliver you to the ski slopes of Sinaia, if you have energy left in reserve. And we hardly have time to mention that it all comes at bargain prices.

◬ *The shiny Financial Plaza overlooking the Dâmboviţa River*

When to go

SEASONS & CLIMATE

Quite simply, when it comes to the weather, Bucharest is a city of extremes. Winters are bitterly cold, with thermometers rarely climbing out of the blue zone from the end of November until the end of March. Snow covers the ground for months on end, and if you are looking for a guaranteed white Christmas then this is the place to come. The city never looks better than immediately after a snowfall, when its rougher edges are given a charming, frosty frame.

If it exists at all, spring is short in Bucharest. April is either an extension of winter, with temperatures to match, or heralds an early summer, and the city's terraces fill up accordingly. Expect blisteringly hot weather from May to September, well over 30°C (86°F) most of the time. Avoid the place in August at all costs, unless a desire to swelter in 40°C (104°F) heat is on your agenda. The city is all but deserted in August anyway; the wise folk of Bucharest head en masse for the mountains or the beach.

By September's end the pendulum swings backs towards winter, and though autumn gets more of a look-in than spring, do not be surprised to still be drinking spritzers outside in late October, or throwing snowballs early in November.

ANNUAL EVENTS
Spring

On 1 March, Romanians mark the coming of spring by handing a *Mărțișor* (a brooch with a red and white thread attached to it) to every woman or girl they know. Visitors are not excused, so buy plenty of *Mărțișor* well in advance; stalls selling them are ubiquitous, especially in the city centre around Piața Română.

⬤ *The Ateneu Român provides a stunning setting for classical concerts*

International Women's Day on 8 March is a big event in Bucharest and the rest of Romania. It's traditional to make a gift of flowers to all the women in your life.

The biggest event of the spring is **Orthodox Easter**, which often falls on a different weekend from the Roman equivalent. Easter is a bigger deal than Christmas in Romania, and many locals – even the young – still keep Lenten vows and attend Easter mass (always held at midnight on Easter Saturday).

May Day is traditionally celebrated either with an outing to the Black Sea coast (regardless of the weather) or by having a barbecue in one of the forests that surround the city, such as Baneasa.

Summer
Churches and monasteries are packed on 15 August as Romanians celebrate the **Assumption of the Virgin Mary**.

Every other September, the **George Enescu Music Festival** at the Ateneu Român celebrates the life and work of Romania's greatest composer, George Enescu, and attracts some of the world's finest musicians.

Autumn
St Dumitru cel Nou (St Dumitru the New) is the patron saint of Bucharest, and is celebrated around 26 October when thousands queue at the Patriarchal Cathedral to view his remains.

Winter
Romania's national holiday is on 1 December and celebrates the unification of Transylvania with Wallachia and Moldavia

in 1918. It is marked with a military parade in front of Arcul
de Triumf.

Christmas is a quiet time in Bucharest, as many of the city's
residents go 'home' to their traditional villages or towns. They
all come back for **New Year's Eve**, however; free concerts are
usually held in both Piaţa Revoluţiei (organised by radio station
Pro FM) and Piaţa Constituţiei (organised by the local council).
The two gigs – which go on long into the night – often feature
the same acts: local bands who flitter from one to the other.

January and February are the main months of the **skiing
season**, although the upper slopes at Sinaia often have snow
well into May.

PUBLIC HOLIDAYS
New Year's Day 1 Jan
Orthodox Easter Sunday 24 Apr 2011; 15 Apr 2012; 5 May 2013
May Day 1 May
National Day 1 Dec
Christmas Day 25 Dec

To the chagrin of its workforce, Romania has precious few
public holidays. While most shops, banks and businesses close,
public transport continues to run, even on Christmas Day.
Restaurants, cafés and bars are usually unaffected, except on
Christmas Day, New Year's Day and Easter Sunday, when the city
shuts down.

The swagger returns

Bucharest in the 1930s had a vibrancy – despite or perhaps even because of the political ambivalence of the times – that until very recently it never looked like recovering. Then of course, in 2007, Romania was made a member of the European Union, and the country got its mojo back; the capital markedly so. The swagger and gentle arrogance of the ancient regime had returned. And just as the 1920s and 30s were marked by the erection of coruscating examples of inter-war architecture that remain startling in their impact today (none more so than the Ambasador Hotel on Bulevardul Magheru, see page 36), so the economic growth between EU accession and the economic crisis saw the construction of bold, confident examples of contemporary architecture. The finest current example of this is the Architectural Union's building on Piața Revoluției (see page 65), a daring glass structure built within the shell of a house destroyed during the revolution.

Yet just as the plethora of glorious architecture that made Bucharest popular in the inter-war years did not seal its status as one of Europe's great cities, nor did the contemporary boom. With that in mind, Bucharest's current administration, led by Mayor Sorin Oprescu, set about creating something special, by reviving the city's historic, neglected centre, around Lipscani. Almost every street in this area is lined with glorious secession architecture, mainly town houses built in art nouveau style at the turn of the 19th century. Most are dilapidated and in need of careful, painstaking renovation. This will happen over many years, as the process will be long (renovation began in earnest only in early 2008) but the fact that the city now has a plan in place to create what would be a living museum of historic importance, is just another sign that Bucharest is shaking off its communist shackles and becoming a thoroughly modern city.

▲ *The innovative Architectural Union building*

History

According to the legend, Bucharest was founded by a shepherd called Bucur, who sat down to rest somewhere close to Piața Obor in the 12th century and liked the look of the place.

The city only really grew after Vlad III Țepeș (Vlad III the Impaler) moved his princely court here in 1459. The city was partially burnt down by the Turks in the 16th century, but it grew again in the early 18th century around the current Lipscani district, which became the busiest trading post in Wallachia.

Occupied by Russians and Austrians for brief periods in the 19th century, Bucharest became the capital of the United Romanian Principalities of Wallachia and Moldavia in 1861, and by 1900 it had a population of 300,000, making it one of Europe's biggest cities. It remained the Romanian capital at the end of World War I (in which Romania fought with the Entente) after Transylvania was united with the principalities.

Romania was split during World War II. Most of Transylvania was awarded to Hungary under the terms of the Molotov–Ribbentrop Pact, while the rest of the country became a quasi-German protectorate. Romanian forces fought with the Nazis on the Eastern Front, and were involved in some of the war's more infamous massacres of Jews.

Wartime leader Ion Antonescu was arrested by the young king, Mihai, on 23 August 1944, and Romania immediately changed sides and supported the Allies. That did not prevent a Soviet invasion, and by 1947 the king had been forced to abdicate and a Stalinist regime installed. The 1950s were marked by subservience to Moscow. After a slight thaw following the election of Nicolae Ceaușescu to head the Communist Party in 1965, the economy collapsed in the 1970s and 1980s, and repression grew. In December 1989 the population exploded in revolution, toppled Ceaușescu and proclaimed a new government. The revolution was quickly hijacked by Ion Iliescu, a former henchman of Ceaușescu, who kept most power in his and his party's hands. Students demonstrating against this situation were brutally killed by miners – staunch Iliescu loyalists – in Piața Universității in June 1990.

Since then Bucharest has been slowly transformed into a modern European capital. Iliescu left the presidency for good in 2004, and most remnants of the old regime left with him. Recent governments have overseen an incredible amount of reform, culminating in the country's accession to the EU on 1 January 2007. Romania's next challenge is to emerge from the recession, which has hit its fragile economy for six, and get back on the path to economic growth.

● *The Central Committee building's balcony, site of Ceaușescu's last speech*

Lifestyle

On the surface, Bucharest is just like any other European capital. The same brand names advertise themselves in bright lights from city-centre rooftops and the city's young population eats sushi, sends texts and has the latest hiphop tune as its ringtone. Expensive cars park haphazardly on pavements with utter disregard for passers-by.

Underneath, however, Bucharest is different. Even the bright young things zooming the city's streets on their trendy mopeds have vague recollections of the recent past, when queuing for basic foodstuffs was a day-to-day activity. The legacy of those days most visible in today's young Bucharest population is the need to do everything instantly; why live for tomorrow? It is this that in many ways gives the city its dynamism. Among the young there is a thirst for everything international: faces often light up at the realisation that you're a foreigner, and many people will go out of their way to help if you ask for directions, seizing a rare chance to practise their English skills in conversation with a native speaker.

The older generation – for whom the memories of communism are far more vivid – gets the past out of its system in a different way. Smart enough to know that time changes nothing, they do absolutely nothing instantly, and leave everything for tomorrow. As this generation still has a monopoly in a number of the service professions, you can expect customer service to be, by and large, poor.

One thing you cannot fail to notice while in town is the devoutness of Romanians of all ages. Look out for the cross the majority of Romanians make when passing a church, and the number of shops selling religious icons to locals. The Romanian Orthodox Church (to which the vast majority of the city's population belongs) had a strange accommodation with the communist regime, but by hook or by crook its reputation survived intact. Since the revolution it has once again become the institution that all age groups most trust and respect. Visiting at any time will give you a sense of this; visiting at Christmas or (especially) Easter will make you feel part of it.

◆ High modern expectations often clash with old-fashioned realism

Culture

Even during the darker years of the communist regime, Bucharest's theatres were full, though fuel shortages meant they often went unheated. The number of working theatres is well into double figures, all with their own unique theatre companies; most are still supported by the state. The National Theatre is one of the city's landmarks; sitting in Piața Universității, its main hall is used for staging everything from musicals to serious drama. As it's all performed in Romanian, however, it is unlikely to tempt the visitor unless he or she is desperate to see *King Lear* in a foreign language. Instead, admire its strange exterior (see page 83) and head for the lively music venue it hosts on the top floor, Laptaria lui Enache, where good young bands of all descriptions play most nights.

More likely to be of interest to you is the Romanian National Opera (see page 87), housed in a fine neoclassical building on Bulevardul Mihai Kogălniceanu. There are performances most days at 18.30, and tickets are cheap. The ballet shares the building, and one performance a week is usually reserved for ballet fans.

Bucharest has recently provided the backdrop for a number of big-money Hollywood films. The high-quality but low-budget production facilities at the former state-run studios out at Buftea (see page 108), along with cheap extras and skilled film technicians, have made film one of the city's most lucrative industries. Romanians in turn love the cinema, and the city boasts several huge multi-screen cinemas, as well as some charmingly old-school state-run outlets with a programme of

⬤ *The plush interior of the National Opera House*

classic film, festival efforts, documentaries and other less mainstream pictures. The good news for visitors is that, in Bucharest, films are shown in the original language with Romanian subtitles. Ticket prices are again cheap, especially if you avoid the glitzy mall cinemas.

Bucharest is also becoming something of a Mecca for lovers of art deco architecture. It seems that even in the most depressing of side streets, the glorious, often faded grandeur of a 1920s masterpiece is ready to jump out at you. Bulevardul Magheru is home to a number of these gems; admire the two typical art deco hotels that stand opposite each other, the Lido and the Ambasador.

You will also find that there is no shortage of bookshops in the city. Romanians read more books than almost any other nation on earth, devouring all sorts of work by their own gifted authors, as well as an increasing amount of translated work by foreign writers. There are a growing number of decent English bookshops too; try **Anthony Frost** (a Calea Victoriei 45), **Cărturesti** (a Str Arthur Verona 13, just off Bul Magheru by Patria Cinema) or the **Libraria Dalles** on Bulevardul Bălcescu. The crazy, chaotic streets of Lipscani also offer hidden first editions in their antique and pawn shops.

⏵ *Row your cares away on the Cişmigiu Garden Lake*

 # MAKING THE MOST OF
Bucharest

Shopping

If you are coming to Bucharest to shop, think again. You will find little here you can't get at home. Brand names that are middle-of-the-road elsewhere are priced as luxury items here.

What you do find, however, is a delightful range of antique shops, as well as specialist places selling unique gifts, such as Romanian Orthodox iconography, glass, naïve art and both communist and Nazi-era memorabilia. If a Lenin statuette takes your fancy, you'll love Obor Market (although things might change soon as the area is due to be re-developed as a mall) or the many antique shops of Lipscani.

The city's main shopping areas are Bulevardul Magheru and Calea Victoriei, where you will find high-end fashion labels, expensive boutiques and a bevy of perfumeries. Eight modern malls now compete to attract the city's shoppers. The most upscale is Baneasa Shopping City (see page 111), outside of the city, which features hundreds of stores, including all the high-street brands you will know from home. Closer to the city centre are the București Mall, Plaza Romania, Liberty Center, AFI Palace Cotroceni, City Mall and Sun Plaza. All offer multi-screen cinemas and fast food joints alongside the shops. Going up a level is the Unirea Shopping Center (see page 83), a sort of post-Communist retail village.

● *The Unirea Shopping Center is a retail Mecca*

USEFUL SHOPPING PHRASES

How much is this?	**Can I try this on?**
Cât costă?	Pot să o (îl) probez?
Cuht costah?	*Pot sah oh (ul) probez?*

My size is ...	**I'll take this one, thank you**
Am mărimea ...	O iau pe aceasta, mulţumesc
Ahm mareemia ...	*Oh iaoo peh acheyasta, mooltzoomesc*

Piaţa Amzei (see page 69) is the city's main produce market, but there are others at Piaţa Obor and Piaţa Dorobanţilor. They mainly sell fresh fruit and vegetables but Obor especially can become something of a flea market at weekends – though this may end once the area's redevelopment is completed.

If you want to take home something exclusively Romanian as a gift or souvenir, you could do worse than the Romanian version of Monopoly, on sale in most of the city's toy shops. You could also go for some Romanian music; the operas and concertos of George Enescu, or some *muzica lautareasca*, as heard at weddings, christenings and parties all over Romania. Look out for CDs by Maria Dragomiroiu and Benone Sinulescu.

In Sinaia, ski shops offer cut-price skis and snowboards from mid-February onwards. Also look out for the craft markets between Sinaia, Buşteni and Azuga; most of the wares are touristy rubbish, but there's also hand-woven lace, wooden children's toys and knitted shepherds' pullovers.

Eating & drinking

Good food in Bucharest is now thankfully very easy to find. In fact, choosing from the plethora of great, good-value eateries will be one of your hardest daily decisions while in town. Every genre is on offer, from traditional Romanian cuisine to cutting-edge fusion, and everything in between.

Romanian food is tasty if unadventurous. Most restaurants serving local specialities will offer you a range of sour soups, known as *ciorbă*, which are full of vegetables and often meals in themselves. *Ciorbă de perisoare* (meatball sour soup) is particularly tasty, though *ciorbă de fasole* (bean sour soup) and *ciorbă de vacuța* (beef sour soup) are also to be recommended. More of an acquired taste is the local favourite, *ciorbă de burta*, made from cows' intestines. After a *ciorbă* try some *sarmale* (cabbage leaves, or sometimes vine leaves, stuffed with meat and rice) served with *mamaliga* (polenta) and covered in sour cream – it is the national dish. Romanians are also fond of large

PRICE CATEGORIES

The following approximate price bands are based on the average cost of a three-course meal for one person, excluding drinks, and are indicated by these symbols:

£ up to 50 lei **££** 50–100 lei **£££** over 100 lei

In even the most expensive restaurants you will be hard pushed to spend more than 150 lei for a good meal, providing you do not go mad with the imported wines.

chunks of meat, such as *ciolan afumat* (pork knuckle) and *costițe* (ribs). Pork and chicken are the staples of the diet, with beef rarely found on menus (except in soups), while lamb is eaten only at Easter. *Mici* (mutton and beef meatballs served with mustard), however, are served in most restaurants and are wonderful, but always best when bought from a street stall. Fish is a disappointment here; expect to find trout, carp and perch on menus, but little else.

When it comes to dessert Romanians have very sweet tastes. Look out for *papanași* (dense little doughnuts covered in cream and syrup) and *clatite* (pancakes) served piping hot with jam

⬤ *A tasty and traditional dish of aubergine salad and bean soup*

EATING OUT

Standards of service can vary, and it is not uncommon
to be entirely ignored by staff after taking your seat. Be
explicit about what exactly you want (confusions occur
often), but don't be surprised if your chosen dish is not
available, even in the best restaurants. A 10 per cent tip is
expected, whether deserved or not, but you will be doing
Romania a disservice by handing out a tip when it has not
been well earned. If you'd rather avoid the hassle and just
sit outdoors with a sandwich, be warned: picnicking in one
of the city's parks could get you shouted at by a guard
(most ideal grassy picnic spots are off limits). Should you
wish to eat on the move, you can pick up picnic supplies
in the city's supermarkets or *alimentară* stores.

or chocolate. Snacks in Bucharest are found on street corners
everywhere; look out for *covrigi* (sweet bread bagels covered
in salt), which are delicious when hot.

There is no shortage of places to drink in Bucharest, from
sophisticated cafés and tea houses to cocktail bars and Irish
pubs. Coffee in Romania is very good, though tea usually means
herbal varieties. Make sure you ask for *ceai negru* if you want
a black tea, and *cu lapte* if you want it with milk.

The local spirit is *țuica*, a highly distilled aperitif made from
grapes or prunes, incredibly strong and an acquired taste. For
a more satisfying taste of Romania try some of the country's
excellent wines. Familiar red grapes such as Merlot and

USEFUL DINING PHRASES

I'd like a table for ... people
Doresc o masă pentru ... persoane
Doresk o masa pentru ... purswahney

Waiter!
Chelner/Chelneriță!
Kelner/Kelnehritsa!

Does this contain meat?
Conține carne?
Kontzyneh carneh?

Could I have the bill, please?
Nota de plată, vă rog?
Notah deh platah, vah rohg?

Where is the toilet, please?
Unde este toaleta, vă rog?
Oondeh este twaleta, vah rohg?

Cabernet Sauvignon have a great tradition in Romania, though quality and price are directly linked; pay as much as you can. White wines are less impressive, though anything on the Chateau Domenii label is worthwhile. You may also like to try the sweet sparkling wine from the Cricova winery in Moldova. Local beer is cheap and good (look out for the Timisoreana, Aurora and Ciucas brands especially), though is losing market share among the city's young folk to imported Danish, German, Belgian and Czech beers.

Entertainment & nightlife

There is no longer any doubt that Bucharest is now well and truly on the European clubbing map. The biggest-name DJs in the world play the city's trendiest clubs at least once a week, with gigs by the very best names on the decks taking place outdoors in summer, or in the enormous Romexpo exhibition centre in winter. Kristal Glam Club (see page 100) started it all off around 2000, paying real money to bring over the biggest names. Now several venues compete for the affections of the city's clubbers. Tickets are rarely sold in advance, and it's first come first served on the door at the venues; get there early. Sometimes, for the very biggest names, it is possible to pre-book tickets. Look out for details in *Bucharest In Your Pocket* (see page 31) or try the website Ⓦ www.bilete.ro

The city is now also starting to play host to top performers. The Rolling Stones, George Michael, Kylie, Madonna, Elton John and Bob Dylan have all played here in recent years as part of their European tours, though the biggest fervour is saved for local favourites such as Depeche Mode. Concerts are sponsored by big corporations, keeping ticket prices refreshingly reasonable. For a taste of the local music scene, however, you might like to try a venue such as Club A (see page 86) or Mojo (see page 87), which has concerts two or three nights a week. Again, tickets are usually sold at the door.

When it comes to more mainstream nightlife, the liveliest district is the old centre, Lipscani, which is now teeming with pubs, bars and clubs. Other quasi 'strips' include the string of cafés along the southern end of Strada Av Radu Beller at Piața

Dorobanților, and Strada Mendeleev around Piața Amzei. The Radu Beller strip is especially popular in summer, when tables are placed in a haphazard and impromptu manner on the pavements outside.

⬤ Bucharest has earned its place on Europe's coolest clubbing list

LISTINGS

Whatever is going on in Bucharest, you'll find details of it in the indispensable English-language bi-monthly *Bucharest In Your Pocket*, available in good hotels, restaurants and expat hangouts all over the city; or the two heavily competing Romanian-language weeklies, *Şapte Seri* and *24-Fun*, plus the local *Time Out*. The first two weeklies can be picked up for free almost anywhere, from McDonald's to metro stations. They also have useful online versions (ⓦ www.sapteseri.ro and ⓦ http://bucuresti.24fun.ro). Though the listings are in Romanian, the cinema schedule is easy enough to understand.

Bucharest is also now a major mover in the world of gambling. You can barely walk down a street in the centre of the city without passing a plush casino. Try the Grand Casinos at the Athénée Palace Hilton or the J W Marriott (see page 39), or the Casino Bucharest at the InterContinental (see page 39).

The other side of Bucharest's nightlife is its seedier, red-light side. Prostitution is illegal in Romania, though women can still be seen loitering by the kerbside at night in certain areas. Tourists will not usually be bothered by the trade, though obviously foreign groups that include young males may be approached on Bulevardul Magheru. Strip clubs are technically legal operations but note that many are merely fronts for unseemly activities and are best avoided.

Sport & relaxation

SPECTATOR SPORTS

Football

The national sport is football. The biggest club is **Steaua Bucharest** (ⓐ Complex Sportiv Steaua, B-dul Ghencea 45 ⓣ 021 411 46 56 ⓦ www.steauafc.com). The other two teams in the capital, **Dinamo** (ⓐ Complex Sportiv Dinamo, Şos Ştefan cel Mare ⓣ 021 210 69 74 ⓦ www.fcdinamo.ro) and **Rapid** (ⓐ Stadion Rapid, Şos Giuleşti ⓣ 021 668 75 55 ⓦ www.fcrapid.ro), are less well supported, but derbies between any of the three are packed-out affairs well worth attending – provided you won't be fazed by the scuffles that often break out. Tickets are cheap and can be bought from the stadiums in advance. The season runs from August to July, with a three-month break from December to March. You can also now buy tickets online, at ⓦ www.bilete.ro

Other sports

The three football clubs above all run teams in a number of other sports, and once again, derbies attract large crowds. Basketball games tend to be played at the **Sala Polivalenta** (ⓐ B-dul Tineretului), ice hockey at the **national ice rink** (ⓐ Patinoar din Complex Sportiv Lia Manoliu, B-dul Basarabiei) and rugby at mini-stadiums behind the football grounds (usually with free entrance). In September, the Romanian Open Tennis Championships are held at the **National Tennis Centre** (ⓐ Str Dr Lister).

For venues and ticket information for all sports, check out the sports newspaper *Gazeta Sporturilor* (ⓦ www.gsp.ro).

◔ The pacy Bănel Nicoliță in action for Steaua Bucharest

PARTICIPATION SPORTS

Bowling

Try **Rock and Roll Bowling** at the Bucureşti Mall (ⓐ Calea Vitan 53–55 ⓛ 10.00–24.00), **Play Planet** at the Plaza Romania (ⓐ B-dul Timişoara 26 ⓛ 10.00–22.00) or **Funland** (see page 46), in the Unirea Shopping Center.

Cycling

Many of the main parks have rental outlets.

Horse-riding

Hipocan (ⓐ Corbeanca ⓣ 0741 100 214 ⓦ www.hipocan.ro) is a well regarded riding club near the airport at Otopeni, with indoor and outdoor facilities.

Ice-skating

At the **Lia Manoliu Rink** (ⓐ B-dul Basarabiei 37–39 ⓣ 021 324 65 35 ⓛ 10.00–16.00, closed for big ice hockey matches) you can hire skates. In winter you can skate on Lake Cişmigiu.

Skiing

Head to Sinaia in the winter for great skiing (see page 121).

Swimming

The major hotels offer pristine swimming pools. In summer try the large and popular **Water Park** (ⓐ Şos Bucureşti-Ploieşti ⓛ 10.00–20.00 Mon–Fri, 09.00–20.00 Sat & Sun ⓦ www.waterpark.ro) opposite Henri Coanda Otopeni airport.

Accommodation

Visitors to the city still tend to be mainly business travellers on expense accounts, and the choice at the sharp end of the market is far greater than at backpacker level. There is nowhere to camp in Bucharest, but there are hostels and a couple of cheap and cheerful bargain hotels. The mid-range market remains something of a void. Those reasonable three-star places that do exist tend to be out of the city centre and quite often fail to reach international standards. You are best advised to spend as much as you can afford.

Note that most parts of Bucharest city centre are very busy and crowded with traffic. For a quiet sleep you are better off in one of the more serene districts, such as the north of the city, although you'll have the expense of taxis into the city centre.

Booking in advance is always a good idea, either through an internet hotel booking site or direct through the hotel. Avoid turning up on spec as you will end up paying the rack rate, which is always at least 30 per cent more expensive than

PRICE CATEGORIES

Note that almost all hotels in Bucharest, and throughout Romania, list their prices in euros (€). The following price guides indicate the approximate cost of a room for two people for one night, including breakfast, VAT and local taxes.

£ up to €100   ££ €100–150   £££ over €150

the pre-booked rate. A buffet breakfast is almost always included in the room rate. Tea and coffee facilities are not always available in rooms, even in the best hotels. Cable television with at least one English news channel is standard in all but the cheapest places, and en-suite bathrooms are pretty much a given; expect a shower but not an actual bath tub. Most hotel staff speak good English.

HOTELS

Ambasador £ Though the somewhat stuffy rooms and services inside the hotel do not match the fabulous art deco building, it has a great location and prices are relatively cheap. ⓐ B-dul Magheru 8–10 ⓣ 021 315 90 80 ⓦ www.ambasador.ro

Das President £ Previously known as the Cerna, this place was renovated in 2008 and now boasts a raft of new amenities such as air-conditioning. ⓐ B-dul Dinicu Golescu 29 ⓣ 021 311 05 35 ⓦ www.daspresident.ro

Piccolo Mondo £ Large rooms, simply but tastefully furnished, above the city's best Lebanese restaurant. A taxi ride from the city centre but great value, and its situation in a residential area means a quiet night's sleep is guaranteed. ⓐ Calea Clucerului 9 ⓣ 021 260 06 82 ⓦ www.piccolomondo.ro

Villa Helga £ Bucharest's only official Hostelling International affiliated hostel, this place offers the cheapest beds in the city, alongside a host of extras, from internet and free breakfast to kitchen and laundry room access. No curfew. ⓐ Str Mihai Eminescu 184 ⓣ 021 212 08 28

Golden Tulip £–££ Just north of Piaţa Revoluţiei, this four-star hotel offers free wireless internet in all its large rooms. A bit characterless, it does have a well-equipped health club, with sauna and whirlpool. ⓐ Calea Victoriei 166 ⓣ 021 212 55 58 ⓦ www.goldentulipbucharest.com

Rembrandt £–££ Best-value place in the city. Great little rooms, all individually furnished with style and panache. Run by friendly Dutch people and with a perfect location in Lipscani. ⓐ Str Smardan 11 ⓣ 021 313 93 15 ⓦ www.rembrandt.ro

El Greco ££ Housed inside a gorgeous neoclassical villa, an exquisite hotel offering luxurious, large rooms at a decent (if not exactly bargain) price. ⓐ Str Jean Louis Calderon 16 ⓣ 021 315 81 31 ⓦ www.hotelelgreco.ro

Opera ££ Good mid-range choice, but noisily close to Piaţa Revoluţiei. The winding staircase up to the rooms is a gem, and the small, well-appointed rooms are good value. ⓐ Str Ion Brezoianu 37 ⓣ 021 312 48 55 ⓦ www.thhotels.ro

Pullman ££ Previously a Sofitel, this four-star place, located north of the centre in the World Trade complex, has large rooms and numerous services. ⓐ Piaţa Montreal 10 ⓣ 021 318 30 00 ⓦ www.accorhotels.com

K&K Elisabeta ££–£££ The Czech Koller brothers' latest hotel is a stunning villa conversion in the city centre. Expect the usual K&K extras, from personal service to antique furniture.
ⓐ Str Slanic 26 ⓣ 021 302 92 80 ⓦ www.kkhotels.co.ro

◗ The welcoming and homely Rembrandt hotel

Novotel City Centre ££–£££ The charm is provided by the entrance, an exact replica of the National Theatre, which stood on the site until bombed by the British in World War II. Modernity and gadgets aplenty inside. Friendly staff and a sensational location make the price worthwhile. ⓐ Calea Victoriei 37B ⓣ 021 308 85 00 ⓦ www.novotel.com

Athénée Palace Hilton £££ Unquestionably the best hotel in the city, it affords luxury at every turn. The view from the rooms overlooking historic Piața Revoluției are worth the extra money they cost. Look out for special deals on the Hilton website. ⓐ Str Episcopiei 1–3 ⓣ 021 303 37 77 ⓦ www.hilton.com

Crowne Plaza £££ The quiet setting away from the city centre makes this a good choice for families. Luxurious rooms, outstanding service and excellent Sunday brunch. ⓐ B-dul Poligrafiei 1 ⓣ 021 224 00 34 ⓦ www.ichotelsgroup.com

InterContinental £££ For almost three decades this was the only five-star hotel in the city. From its balconies journalists reported live on the revolution taking place below in December 1989. ⓐ B-dul Nicolae Bălcescu 2–4 ⓣ 021 310 20 20 ⓦ www.intercontinental.com

J W Marriott £££ Its location just outside the main action gives the opulent Marriott a spaciousness that some of its more central five-star competitors lack. ⓐ Calea 13 Septembrie 90 ⓣ 021 403 10 00 ⓦ www.marriott.com

THE BEST OF BUCHAREST

Bucharest offers a surprising mix of fascinating museums, grand palaces and unusual architecture. You can kick back in one of the tranquil parks, or just sit with a coffee and take in the city's vibrant atmosphere.

TOP 10 ATTRACTIONS

- **Casa Poporului** Ceaușescu's folly; a huge, imposing building known as 'House of the People' (see page 74).

- **Muzeul Satului (Village Museum)** An open-air museum showcasing the best of the architecture of the Romanian countryside (see page 93).

- **Muzeul Țăranului Român (Peasant Museum)** Bucharest's best museum hosts fascinating exhibitions and organises craft and arts workshops (see page 95).

- **Herăstrău Park** Bucharest's largest park with lakes, paths, playgrounds, cafés and terraces (see page 89).

- **Nights out in Lipscani** Once a down-at-heel no-go area, Bucharest's old town has emerged as a buzzing nightlife hub, heaving with hip bars and quirky cafés (see page 78).

- **Muzeul Național de Artă (National Art Museum)** All of Romania's best-known artists have work exhibited here, from painter Nicolae Grigorescu to sculptor Constantin Brâncuși (see page 66).

- **Curtea Veche (Old Court Church & Palace)** Bucharest first developed as a city around the 15th-century court palace, now no more than ruins (see page 75).

- **La Strada at the Athénée Palace** Since the 1920s the great and good have drunk coffee here and watched the world go by (see page 70).

- **Muzeul de Istorie al Evreilor din România (Jewish History Museum)** Half of Romania's Jews died in the Holocaust. This museum commemorates them (see page 82).

- *Covrigi* If you're lucky enough to get a piping hot one, you will be hooked for life on these simple but tasty bagels (see page 27).

▼ *The relaxing green space of Herăstrău Park*

Suggested itineraries

HALF-DAY: BUCHAREST IN A HURRY

You'll have enough time to whizz around Casa Poporului and see the main sights of the city centre on foot. Start at Casa Poporului and join the tour of the building. Walk along Bulevardul Unirii to the enormous Piața Unirii, taking a left onto Bulevardul Ion C Bratianu. Near here are the remains of the princely court, the city's oldest building. A short walk uphill past the Old Court Church brings you to the lovely jumble of old shops that is Lipscani; there are numerous places to stop for a coffee. Pass the National Bank and head for the onion-domed Russian Church. Just ahead is the main building of Bucharest University and the historically important Piața Universității.

1 DAY: TIME TO SEE A LITTLE MORE

After following the half-day itinerary and allowing a little more time for browsing the antique shops of Lipscani and popping into one of its cafés for refreshments, take a walk north from Piața Universității along Bulevardul Magheru, paying special attention to the glorious art deco architecture of the Lido and Ambasador hotels. Turn left as you pass the Lido, and head for Piața Revoluției. After an outdoor lunch at Trattoria Il Calcio (see page 69), admire the abstract revolution monument and spend an hour in the National Art Museum. The collection of religious art on the first floor is the main attraction here. You'll then need to hail a cab to visit the enchantingly non-urban Village Museum. Head next door to Herăstrău Park to enjoy the host of terraces and restaurants on the shore of Lake Herăstrău.

2–3 DAYS: TIME TO SEE MUCH MORE

The extra time would allow you to enjoy the suggestions opposite in a more leisurely manner, then fit in visits to the Peasant Museum, the Jewish Museum and Cişmigiu Garden. The Botanical Gardens are a half-day trip in themselves, while Lake Snagov and Mogoşoaia Palace are full-day trips, including a picnic or barbecue lunch. At night make sure you sample the city's top restaurants and bars.

LONGER: ENJOYING BUCHAREST TO THE FULL

You can do all the above and still have time to experience the full Top 10 Attractions list. One entire day can be spent just enjoying the bustle and life of the city centre, browsing the shops of Magheru and Calea Victoriei. There will also be the chance to head out to Sinaia for a day or two's skiing or mountain walking (depending on the time of year), and to visit Sinaia Monastery and Peleş Castle.

● Wander through the historic Lipscani district

Something for nothing

All of Bucharest's churches are free to enter, though all have small donation boxes at the entrance; just give what you can. Another way of donating is to do as the locals do, and buy a candle and light it in memory of a loved one. The best churches are the Kretulescu Church on Piața Revoluției, which has been fully renovated inside and out, and the tiny but gorgeous Small White Church close by on Calea Victoriei. A little further away is the Russian Church on Strada Ion Ghica, whose onion domes are a feature of the city. Back on Piața Revoluției it costs nothing to go inside the Ateneu Român and to admire its fine lobby, while the National Art Museum opposite is free on the first Wednesday of every month. For glorious free views of the communist-era city centre, take the lift or escalators to the top floor of the Unirea Shopping Center on Piața Unirii.

All of Bucharest's parks and green spaces (except the Botanical Gardens) are free, and the well-kept gardens and paths of Cișmigiu Garden make it a great place to escape the city bustle and take a rest on one of its characteristic benches. If you are a decent chess player you can challenge the experts who congregate here from dawn to dusk, regardless of the weather. Be warned though, the standard is high!

For a taste of the real Romania, head for the enormous Piața Obor, where all kinds of life, from card sharks to Roma people in full traditional, colourful regalia, congregate. You will find everything imaginable on sale here, from fresh fruit and vegetables to spare parts for old Romanian cars. The real fun though is watching real Romanians living real lives, such as old women haggling over the price of potatoes, or taking part in mini-auctions of live chickens and ducks. For maximum effect come in the morning when the market is at its busiest. The area is currently being redeveloped, so visit before it all changes.

🔺 *The impressive exterior of the National Art Museum*

When it rains

There is no getting away from the fact that Bucharest is miserable when it rains. All of the churches and museums can be visited in a shower, though they are some distance away from each other so it's worth selecting one and exploring it thoroughly. Walking the city can be unpleasant as its poor drainage system means that water sits on the road surface, making some streets – even in the city centre – impassable for pedestrians (unless you want very wet feet) after the merest of downpours. You'll therefore be constantly calling taxis, so try and head for places that can fill up more than an hour or two at a time; the Casa Poporului, the Peasant Museum and the National Art Museum are good choices.

Another suggestion is a visit to one of the city's big shopping malls (see page 23). There you will find multi-screen cinemas, bowling alleys, children's play areas, a choice of cafés and restaurants and enough shops to keep you happy for a wet morning or afternoon.

If you get caught in a shower while in the city centre and a cab will not stop, dive into an appealing café or the English Bar at the Hilton (see page 73), where you will be able to spend a couple of glorious hours drinking coffee (or something stronger) and reading.

Further suggestions for rainy days include swimming (see page 34), or **Funland** (ⓐ Piaţa Unirii ❶ 021 303 04 60 ⓦ www.funlandromania.ro ❶ 10.00–24.00 daily) on the top floor of the Unirea Shopping Center. It offers ten-pin bowling, pool tables, a huge children's play area, fast food restaurants, cafés and a licensed bar.

⬤ *The St Nicholas (Russian) Church is well worth a visit*

On arrival

TIME DIFFERENCE
Bucharest is two hours ahead of Greenwich Mean Time (GMT) and British Summer Time (BST).

ARRIVING
By air
Bucharest has two international airports. If you arrive by scheduled flight with British Airways or with Romania's national airline, Tarom, you will land at Henri Coanda Otopeni International Airport, 17 km (10½ miles) from the city centre. It's small but has all the basic facilities: ATMs, bureaux de change (which should be avoided due to the high commission), car hire and cafés.

Avoid the taxi touts at the exit as they will certainly rip you off. One option is to head instead for the blue and grey Fly Taxi people carriers that sit outside the arrivals terminal. A ride to the city centre will cost around 130 lei. A better-value alternative is either to walk to the departures terminal and pick up a cab that is dropping other passengers off, or call a trustworthy taxi company (see page 56) and arrange to meet the driver in the car park opposite the building.

It is cheaper still to take the airport bus 783 that stops in front of the domestic flight terminal. Tickets cost around 8 lei and are valid for the return journey too. Buy them in the silver kiosk next to the bus stop before boarding. The bus runs from around 05.30 to 23.00 and stops at Piața Victoriei, Piața Română and Piața Universității, terminating at Piața Unirii.

Bucharest's second airport is Aurel Vlaicu International Airport, 10 km (6 miles) from the city centre. It is used mainly by budget airlines and is basic. There is an ATM, however, and some car hire desks. Bus 133 to Piaţa Română is the best way to get into town. Tickets cost around 1.50 lei and need to be bought from the kiosks opposite the airport before boarding, then stamped once you are on the bus (see page 53).

By rail
Gara de Nord is modelled on the famous Gare du Nord in Paris, and is the only train station in the city that travellers are ever likely to use. Its facilities include left luggage (🕒 06.00–24.00), ATMs, a café, a **McDonald's** (🕒 07.00–24.00), newsstands and a shop. Taxis wait outside (see page 56). The city centre is also accessible by metro: Piaţa Victoriei is a short ride from Gara de Nord on Ⓜ metro line M1. Trolleybus 85 runs from outside the station to Piaţa Universităţii.

🔺 The towering InterContinental hotel is a useful landmark

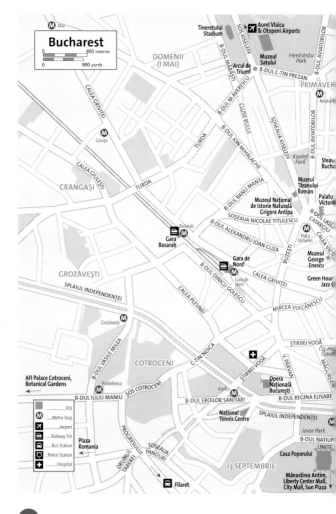

By road
Filaret Bus Station (ⓐ Piața Gării Filaret 1 ❶ 021 336 06 92
ⓦ www.autogari.ro) is slightly out of the city centre and has
no ATM or left luggage, or much of anything else. The only way
to get to the city centre from Filaret is to chance a taxi or catch
ⓝ bus: 232 to Piața Unirii (if the kiosk selling bus tickets is open).

FINDING YOUR FEET
Bucharest is a remarkably safe city. The biggest dangers to
pedestrians are posed by drivers disregarding road rules, and
the city's population of around 100,000 street dogs (see page
129). While major boulevards and streets are clearly signposted,
side streets can go entirely unmarked. The numbering of
buildings also leaves a lot to be desired, so a good map is useful.

ORIENTATION
Bucharest's biggest problem for tourists is that it lacks a
single, genuine city centre; Piața Universității, Piața Unirii and
Piața Română all compete for that title. The best focal point
is probably Piața Universității, as its InterContinental hotel is
visible from much of the city. As a guide, keep a mental note of
where you are in relation to Calea Victoriei, the city's main
north–south thoroughfare.

GETTING AROUND
Buses, trolleybuses & trams
Bucharest has invested heavily in buses, and most lines through
the city centre are now served by modern, wide buses. They are
often still overcrowded, however, and many have no air

IF YOU GET LOST, TRY ...

Do you speak English?
Vobiţi engleześte?
Vorbeetz englezeshteh?

Where is ...?
Unde este ...?
Oondeh esteh ...?

Can you point to it on my map?
Puteţi să-mi arătaţi pe harta?
Pootetz sah-mee arahatz pe hartah?

conditioning in summer. The city also has a network of trams and trolleybuses, but they are painfully slow and only skirt the city centre. In fact, most tourists tend to avoid public transport altogether – taxis are so cheap in Bucharest that even the most penny-pinching backpacker can afford them. However, if you do wish to brave the buses, trams or trolleybuses, the ticketing system for all three is the same; you need to purchase a ticket from a silver kiosk marked *Bilete RATB* before boarding. Once on board frank the ticket in the contraptions attached to the vehicle. On-the-spot fines for being caught without a valid, franked ticket are high. Not all stops have ticket booths, so stock up when you get the chance.

Metro
Bucharest's relatively new metro system was built primarily to ship workers out to the huge industrial estates on the edge of the city. Although maps are few and far between, the system

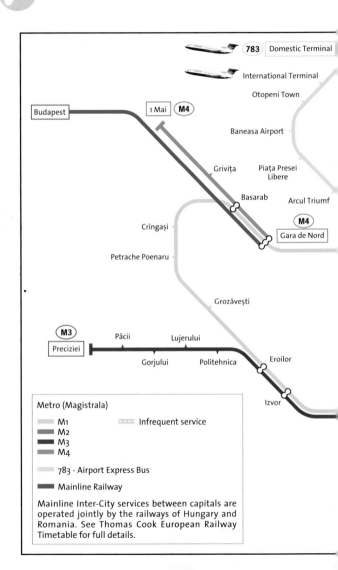

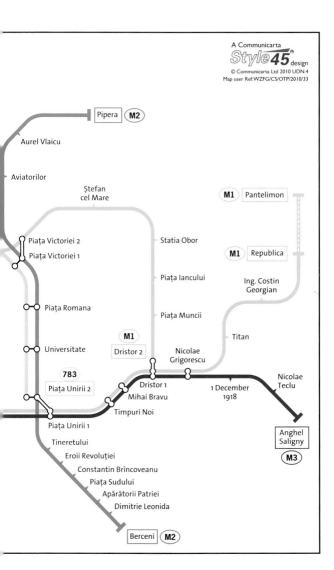

is simple to fathom and the metro is often the cheapest and most efficient way of crossing the city north or southwards. Tickets are purchased at station entrances, and they need to be franked at the platform entrance.

Taxis

Most Bucharest taxis (all of which are painted yellow) are honest and cheap. Stick to a taxi from a trusted company (see below) and you will be OK. Problems are posed by unscrupulous privateers who overcharge. The good news is that tariffs have to be displayed on the taxi door. Do not pay more than about 2 lei per kilometre (Fly Taxis charge more). Ensure the meter is running before setting off.

As ☎ 021 9435
Cristaxi ☎ 021 9461/6
Getax ☎ 021 9531
Meridian ☎ 021 9444
Perrozzi ☎ 021 9631

Car Hire

Car hire in Bucharest is now better value than it used to be, though beware of hidden extras.

Avis ⓦ www.avis.ro
Europcar ⓦ www.ahl-autorent.ro
Hertz ⓦ www.hertz.com.ro

◗ *The National Savings Bank is an architectural highlight*

THE CITY OF
Bucharest

Around Piața Revoluției

Piața Revoluției is where the primary events of the Romanian revolution took place, and it can in many ways be regarded as the soul of the city. It is the perfect place to begin exploring Bucharest. A large and open square, it straddles Calea Victoriei, the city's main north–south artery, and is surrounded by historic buildings on all sides, including the landmark Athénée Palace Hilton, the Ateneu Român concert hall, the former Royal Palace, the former Central Committee building, and the Humanitas bookstore, complete with bullet holes from those dramatic events of December 1989. A number of smart and pleasant side streets host boutiques and trendy restaurants, while the bustle of Piața Amzei, the city centre's biggest market, is a short walk north. A couple of hundred metres in the other direction is the far quieter Cișmigiu Garden, a genuine oasis of calm.

SIGHTS & ATTRACTIONS

Athénée Palace Hilton

So much has gone on in the near-century since the Athénée Palace was opened that a former American diplomat, Rosie Waldeck, based in Bucharest during World War II, wrote a book – *Athene Palace* – about the intrigues, espionage and double dealings that went on here throughout the 1930s and 1940s. At the time this was the only luxury hotel in the city, and anyone of any importance who came to Bucharest stayed here. The building itself, though much renovated since its completion in 1912, retains its original late secession profile – note the ironwork of the balconies – with some early art deco squiggles added later. Inside, the lobby is neoclassical, with marble columns and a sublime ballroom. If there are no events going on, the staff allow visitors to take a look round. Keep an eye out for the sepia photos placed all over the building showing how various sections and rooms looked half a century ago. Top your visit off with a peep at the English Bar, which is in a small room at the back of the hotel; it's open to non-guests. The bar features heavily in Olivia Manning's *Balkan Trilogy*. ⓐ Str Episcopiei 1–3

🔺 *The Athénée Palace Hilton is a living vestige of Bucharest's history*

Around Piața Revoluției

0   400 metres
0   400 yards

Bulevardul Magheru & Piața Română

A two-minute walk east of Piața Amzei is Bulevardul Magheru, home to shops and banks, offices and hotels, and some of the city's most expensive apartment blocks. The boulevard is busy night and day, and the smell and noise of traffic are overwhelming at rush hour. The boulevard's northern end tips out at Piața Română, more traffic junction than public square, but home to the glorious and slightly dilapidated ASE, the economics faculty of Bucharest University, built in 1929 to the designs of Romanian architect Gregory Cerchez.

Fosta Cladire a Comitetului Central al Partidului Comunist Român (Former Central Committee building)

It was from the balcony of this enormous 1950s building, constructed to house the Communist Party Central Committee, that communist dictator Nicolae Ceaușescu made his last public speech to the Romanian people on 21 December 1989. He fled with his wife the next day by helicopter from the roof as revolutionaries ransacked the lower floors. After the revolution and the disbandment of the Communist Party the building served for over a decade as the Romanian Senate, but since that body moved to the Casa Poporului in 2004 it has stood more or less empty. It is closed to the public. ⓐ Piața Revoluției

Grădina Cișmigiu (Cișmigiu Garden)

Though invariably referred to as Cișmigiu Park, this is officially a garden, laid out to the designs of Austrian landscape artist Carl Meyer from 1845 to 1860. Meyer brought in more than 30,000 trees, plants and shrubs from all over Romania to showcase the diverse flora of the country. Cişmigiu is busy all day every day; its long gladed walkways provide a superb backdrop for strollers. On weekends the place truly buzzes, with yelps and screams from the children's playgrounds alongside the contented murmurs of quieter pursuits, such as chess or rowing on the artificial lake. The lake is frozen in winter and becomes a natural ice rink; skate hire is available. Throughout the year, terraces and cafés serve coffee, drinks and cakes. ⓐ Between B-dul Regina Elisabeta, Calea Victoriei, Str Ştirbei Vodă and B-dul Schiţu Măgureanu ⓛ 24 hours daily

Muzeul Naţional de Artă (National Art Museum building)

The vast majority of this fine, neoclassical building dates from 1812, when a rich merchant, Dinicu Golescu, had it built as a private home. His sons squandered their inheritance and sold it to the Romanian state in 1853. After Alexandru Ioan Cuza was elected to be first prince of the United Romanian Principalities in 1859, it became the Royal Palace, and was the main residence of all of Romania's kings: Carol I, Ferdinand, Carol II and Mihai. In 1944 the cabinet of wartime leader Ion Antonescu was arrested inside, triggering Romania's switch to the Allies' side. Since 1955 it has been the home of Romania's National Art Museum (see page 66). ⓐ Calea Victoriei 49–53 ⓣ 021 313 30 30 ⓦ www.mnar. arts.ro ⓛ 11.00–19.00 Wed–Sun, May–Sept; 10.00–18.00 Wed–Sun, Oct–Apr; closed Mon & Tues

Piaţa Amzei

A short walk north of the Athénée Palace, along Calea Victoriei, Str Piaţa Amzei leads you to the vibrant atmosphere of Piaţa

⬥ *Piața Amzei: for all the fresh fruit and vegetables you could wish for*

Amzei, the city's busiest market. You can buy fresh fruit and vegetables, fish, meat, flowers and all kinds of household gadgets you never knew you needed. Alternatively, just sip coffee in a café and watch a lively and genuine street market at work.

Piaţa Revoluţiei

Today this is little more than a large open square of busy roads and car parks. On 21–22 December 1989, however, it was the scene of pitched battles between revolutionaries and security forces loyal to Ceauşescu. The bullet holes above the Humanitas bookshop on the south side are genuine, left as a memorial to the dead. A more obvious memorial is the Revolution Monument in the middle of the square. Meant to signify freedom breaking through barbed wire, locals say it looks more like an olive on a cocktail stick. Look out for the glass office building (the headquarters of the Bucharest Architectural Union), built within the wrecked shell of a house destroyed in the fighting.

CULTURE

Biserica Creţulescu (Creţulescu Church)

The most famous church in the city, and one of the oldest, it was built in 1720 by Iordache Creţulescu, a leading figure in the Romanian cultural awakening of the 1700s. Damaged during the fighting in 1989, it has recently been restored to exquisite condition, and most of the original frescoes remain remarkably intact. The finest are those on the doors, painted in 1858 by Gheorghe Tattarescu. ⓐ Calea Victoriei 47 ⓛ 07.00–18.00 daily

Muzeul George Enescu (George Enescu Museum)

George Enescu was Romania's greatest composer, though he is
perhaps better known in the Western world as a music teacher;
he was the instructor of legendary violinist Yehudi Menuhin.
The house was built in the first decade of the 20th century, and
betrays the French Baroque preferences of its architect, Ion
Berindei. It's worth visiting for the luxurious interiors of what
is probably the finest private house ever built in Bucharest.
ⓐ Calea Victoriei 141 ⓣ 021 318 14 50 ⓦ www.georgeenescu.ro
ⓛ 10.00–17.00 Tues–Sun, closed Mon ⓘ Admission charge

Muzeul Național de Artă (National Art Museum)

There are three permanent exhibitions in this vast art museum
(see page 63), and all are worthwhile. On the first floor you will
find medieval Romanian art, featuring icons, altars and frescoes
from a number of churches and monasteries, plus one of
Romania's oldest Bibles. The second floor shows modern
Romanian art, with works by all the Romanian 19th- and 20th-
century greats, including painters Nicolae Grigorescu, Theodor
Aman and Gheorghe Tattarescu. On the third floor is a small
but decent collection of 20th-century European art. ⓐ Calea
Victoriei 49–53 ⓣ 021 313 30 30 ⓛ 11.00–19.00 Wed–Sun,
May–Sept; 10.00–18.00 Wed–Sun, Oct–Apr; closed Mon & Tues
ⓘ Admission charge

Sala Palatului

Behind (and attached via a walkway to) the National Art Museum is
the Sala Palatului, famous among architects the world over for its
unusual and gravity-defying concave roof. Constructed in the 1950s,

◔ *Admire the art nouveau splendour of the George Enescu Museum*

the building was used during the communist period to house the Romanian version of a parliament, the National Assembly. It is today used for concerts, theatre productions and musicals. Check the box office, down the steps to the side of the building, for forthcoming attractions. ⓐ Piaţa Palatului ⓣ 021 310 15 22 ⓦ www. sala palatului.ro ⓛ Box office: 10.00–18.00 Mon–Fri, closed Sat & Sun

RETAIL THERAPY

Casa del Habano Possibly the finest selection of genuine Cuban cigars in Europe. The knowledgeable and professional staff will help you choose the perfect cigar, or a gift from a wide range of smoking accessories. ⓐ Str Episcopiei 1–3 (Athénée Palace Hilton) ⓣ 021 311 1581 ⓦ www.lacasadelhabano.ro ⓛ 10.00–22.00 Mon–Sat, 12.00–19.00 Sun

Humanitas Besides books, the main interest for the visitor in this treasure trove will be the vast range of reproduction Orthodox religious icons, from conventional tempera on wood to more modern glass and naïve art icons. ⓐ Calea Victoriei 45 ⓣ 021 313 50 35 ⓦ www.libhumanitas.ro ⓛ 08.30–18.00 Mon–Fri, 09.00–14.00 Sat, closed Sun

Magazin Filatelic The official stamp shop of the Romanian Post Office. A wide range of antique and modern stamps, many portraying scenes from Romania's history. Communist-era stamps are usually the most sought after and expensive. ⓐ Str Ion Câmpineanu 27 ⓣ 021 313 88 96 ⓦ www.romfilatelia.ro ⓛ 08.00–20.00 Mon–Fri, 09.00–12.00 Sat, closed Sun

Piața Amzei The finest fresh fruit, vegetables and flowers that Romania has to offer. You can haggle if you know a little Romanian, but be warned: the old ladies behind the stalls know how to bargain. The area is in the process of being redeveloped, so a reduced selection of stalls may be in operation. ⓐ Str Piața Amzei, near Piața Română ⓑ Most stalls sunrise–sunset daily

Romartizana A wide range of exquisite arts and crafts, all made by skilled Romanian craftsmen. Look out for the glass, lace, tablecloths and carved wooden figures. Mainstream souvenirs are here too, including dolls in national costume and Romanian flags. ⓐ Calea Victoriei 16–20 ⓣ 021 313 14 65 ⓦ www.romartizana.com.ro ⓑ 10.00–20.00 Mon–Fri, 09.00–13.00 Sat, closed Sun

TAKING A BREAK

IO Espresso £ ❶ In the shell of a house destroyed during the revolution the Bucharest Architectural Union built their unique headquarters, and opened up the ground floor as a smart but reasonably priced café. ⓐ Str Demetri Dobrescu 5 ⓣ 021 315 60 98 ⓑ 09.30–last customer Mon–Fri, 10.00–24.00 Sat & Sun

Trattoria Il Calcio £ ❷ Good, simple Italian food (including excellent pizza) in the best location anywhere in the city. ⓐ Str Franklin 1–3 ⓣ 0732 52 81 40 ⓦ www.trattoriailcalcio.ro ⓑ 12.00–24.00 daily

Caffe Frappe £–££ ❸ Huge windows make this the perfect spot to watch the bustle of Piața Amzei while sipping one of the city's better espressos. A little showy in high summer, and later in the evenings, when the 'in' crowd turns up. ⓐ Str Mendeleev 7–15, Piața Amzei ① 021 319 69 21 ① 09.00–24.00 daily

La Strada ££ ❹ The best and most famous terrace in the city, perhaps even country, is this legend at the Athénée Palace. The food is great, the service exemplary and the prices far lower than people expect. The terrace is currently being renovated. ⓐ Athénée Palace Hilton, Str Episcopiei 1–3 (access from Calea Victoriei) ① 021 303 37 77 ① 12.00–01.30 daily May–Sept (weather permitting)

Geisha £££ ❺ Trendy beyond words, this is one for the sunglasses crowd who seem to do little except stay here all day. Casual but wealthy visitors should stop by to see how Romania's rich set live. ⓐ Str C A Rosetti 10 ① 021 315 72 98 ① 08.00–01.00 daily

Turabo £££ ❻ Serving cakes to die for, Turabo attracts a wide range of patrons, from students and backpackers to Romania's jet set. Despite the prices it's up there as the city's best café. ⓐ Str Episcopiei 6 ⓦ www.turabo-cafe.ro ① 08.00–01.00 daily

AFTER DARK

RESTAURANTS
Bistro Ateneu £ ❼ A safe first stop for foreigners wanting to 'go Romanian' – but not *too* Romanian – this lively place has

recently opened its second branch near the George Enescu Museum. The atmosphere remains the same: think 1920s bistro, blackboard menus and live music. ❷ Str Gheorghe Manu 16 ❶ 021 212 77 88 ❾ www.bistronet.ro ❿ 12.00–00.30 daily

Byblos ££ ❽ This fantastic Italian restaurant serves real trattoria food in an unfussy setting at prices that are worth paying, if not entirely cheap. Staff are friendly and the atmosphere clubby. It is great for larger groups. ❷ Str Nicolae Golescu 14–16 ❶ 021 313 20 91 ❾ www.byblos.uv.ro ❿ 12.00–last customer daily

Menuet ££ ❾ Unpretentious food in a small, lively cellar setting near Piaţa Revoluţiei. Food is Hungarian with the odd nod to other eastern European cuisines. ❷ Str Nicolae Golescu 14 ❶ 021 312 01 43 ❾ www.bistromenuet.ro ❿ 12.30–00.30 daily

Balthazar £££ ❿ Bucharest's best restaurant for almost a decade, and still very little real competition in sight. The food on an ever-changing and evolving fusion menu always includes new flavours. It's certainly not cheap, but if you avoid alcohol and choose your food carefully a meal here is by no means as budget-blowing as you might expect. ❷ Str Dumbrava Rosie 2 ❶ 021 212 14 60 ❾ www.balthazar.ro ❿ 12.30–00.30 daily

Bluu £££ ⓫ Housed in a lovely villa, this trendy newcomer has an appealing Italian-inspired menu and is big on presentation. The terrace is the best spot in the warmer months.

ⓐ Str Biserica Amzei 30 ⓣ 021 311 07 01 ⓦ www.bluu.ro
ⓛ 09.00–24.00 daily

Casa Vernescu £££ ⑫ A casino and restaurant where the
French food is good, but it is the surroundings – a historic house
on Bucharest's premier street – that people come for. ⓐ Calea
Victoriei 133 ⓣ 021 311 97 44 ⓦ www.casavernescu.ro
ⓛ 18.30–24.00 daily

La Mandragora £££ ⑬ The German chef at this inventive modern
European restaurant offers daring combinations of ingredients,
which seem to delight the discerning Bucharest public. ⓐ Str
Mendeleev 29 ⓣ 021 319 75 92 ⓦ www. lamandragora.ro
ⓛ 18.00–23.00 Mon–Fri, 18.00–23.30 Sat, closed Sun

Roberto's £££ ⑭ The Hilton's superlative Italian restaurant,
held by many to be the city's best, is getting a facelift in 2011.
Afterwards, expect more of the same: faultless service, a serene
ambience and a regularly changing menu with inventive
delights from Italy. ⓐ Athénée Palace Hilton, Str Episcopiei 1–3
ⓣ 021 303 37 77 ⓛ 11.00–02.00 daily

BARS & CLUBS

Déjà vu If you've no objection to the dubious characters who
congregate at the doorway, or women dancing on the bar while
you're trying to order a drink, Déjà vu offers an unusual and
quintessentially eastern European experience. The music includes
high-energy Romanian and Russian. ⓐ B-dul Nicolae Balcescu 25
ⓣ 021 311 23 22 ⓦ www.dejavu-club.ro ⓛ 20.00–last customer daily

English Bar Mellow and historic, this is the only bar in the city to have a leading role in a novel: Olivia Manning's *Balkan Trilogy*. Comfy leather seats and friendly staff await, as do the expat regulars who swear by the place. ⓐ Athénée Palace Hilton, Str Episcopiei 1–3 ⓣ 021 303 37 77 ⓛ 11.00–01.30 daily

The Office Established in 1998 and still the best club in the city centre. Expect an eclectic mix of music, a wealthy but not extravagant crowd, a great range of imported wine and champagne, and the best dancers in Bucharest. Dress well if you want to get in. ⓐ Str Tache Ionescu 2 ⓣ 0745 11 00 64 ⓦ www.theoffice.ro ⓛ 21.30–05.00 Fri & Sat, 22.00–02.00 Sun

ARTS VENUES

Ateneu Român This stunning concert hall was built in 1888, and has hosted the city's finest orchestras ever since. Today it plays host to the George Enescu Philharmonic, which performs classical concerts most evenings. The best and most popular concerts take place on Fridays, when booking in advance is a must. ⓐ Str Franklin 1 ⓣ 021 315 25 67 ⓦ www.fge.org.ro ⓛ Box office: 10.00–12.00, 16.00–18.30 Mon–Fri, 10.00–12.00 Sat & Sun

Green Hours 22 Jazz Café Jazz, and good jazz at that. There are concerts most nights of the week in this gorgeous little venue in a courtyard off Calea Victoriei. You need to make reservations for the more popular concerts at weekends. Mondays are given over to experimental theatre, and there are often art exhibitions here too. ⓐ Calea Victoriei 120 ⓣ 0722 234 356 ⓦ www.greenhours.ro ⓛ 24 hrs daily

Universitate, Lipscani & Unirii

Piața Universității (known as Universitate) is a city centre in the making. At the moment, however, it remains a phenomenally busy junction. Crossing it involves using the metro underpass, a formerly grotty subway which has emerged from extensive renovation as a shiny new destination, replete with temporary art and design exhibitions, a café, interactive exhibits and – finally – a tourist information centre. It is the gateway to the most interesting parts of the city, and its main landmark, the InterContinental Hotel, is a good beacon if you get lost. The National Theatre is here too, and the city's most picture-postcard church stands on the square's fringes. Piața Unirii is the result of decades of central planning, a vast expanse of concrete designed for the new socialist man Nicolae Ceaușescu claimed to be attempting to create. Linking Universitate and Unirii is the quirky Lipscani district, all that is left of old Bucharest, which has undergone an astonishing renaissance in the last couple of years.

SIGHTS & ATTRACTIONS

Biserica Studenților Sf Nicolae (St Nicholas (Russian) Church)
Built with donations from Russian Tsar Nicholas II in 1904–9, this church – known as the Russian Church – is famous for its onion domes and gold-leaf trimmings. ❸ Str Ion Ghica 9

Casa Poporului (House of the People)
Romania's best-known landmark is the infamous Casa Poporului. It was designed to be the crowning achievement in the life and

career of Ceaușescu, who demolished thousands of houses, tens of churches, a stadium, a monastery and two hospitals to make way for it. Construction began in 1984, and at the time of the dictator's death in 1989 it was all but completed. It has been claimed to be the second-largest building in the world (after the Pentagon). It is certainly big; the building is almost 100 m (328 ft) high and more than 3 km (2 miles) in circumference. Today it hosts the Romanian Parliament, the Senate and the Museum of Contemporary Art. ⓐ Calea 13 Septembrie 1, entrance A3 ⓣ 021 311 36 11 ⓛ 10.00–15.45 daily; sometimes closed for private functions ⓘ Admission charge

Curtea Veche (Old Court Church & Palace)

Bucharest first became important when Vlad III Țepeș moved his court here in the 1450s and built a princely palace. Most of the palace was destroyed by fires in the 19th century. The exquisitely preserved church next door is the oldest in the city (1545). ⓐ Str Franceză ⓛ 10.00–18.00 Tues–Sun, closed Mon

🔺 The Casa Poporului is one of the city's most popular attractions

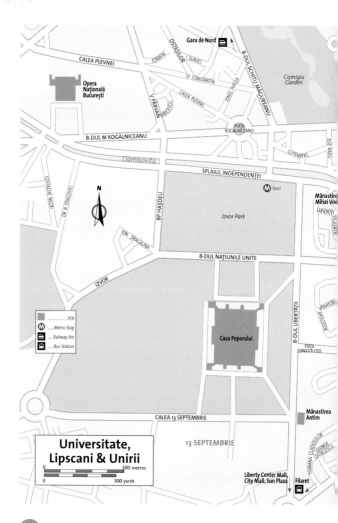

Hanul cu Tei

Han in Romanian means *inn*, and Bucharest was once full of places like this, where traders and travellers could rest their horses in the stables, enjoy a drink and a meal and even stay the night. The Hanul cu Tei (Inn Under the Trees) is today one of the few inns that remain intact, though its purpose has long changed. Instead of highwaymen and their horses, you will instead find the best selection of art and craft workshops and outlets in Bucharest (see page 83). ❸ Str Lipscani 63–65 ❶ 021 313 01 81 Ⓦ www.hanulcutei.ro ❻ 09.00–18.00 Mon–Fri, 09.00–14.00 Sat & Sun

Lipscani

Strada Lipscani is actually one street that runs through the heart of Old Bucharest, but it has lent its name to the whole historic area. According to legend, traders from Leipzig pitched here one day in the 17th century and left their name, Leipzig, becoming, over the years, Lipscani. Today the area is all that survives of the old city, which grew up around the princely court which Vlad III Țepeș moved here in the 15th century.

Much of the dilapidated but clearly glorious architecture of its houses – many built for rich merchants in secession style at the turn of the 20th century, when the area first became really fashionable – gives an idea as to how the whole city must have once looked. It is a great area to explore, and surprises lurk at every corner, from the enormous neoclassical National Bank at Strada Lipscani 25 to the remains of the old princely court itself on Strada Franceză. In recent years the district has been reinvented as Bucharest's major nightlife zone.

Mănastirea Antim (Antim Monastery)

The patriarch of the Orthodox Church, Antim Ivreanul, had this monastery built in 1708 and gave it his name. It is topped by a stunning gold-plated dome, and its church is fronted by carved wooden doors, the work of Ivreanul himself. Inside there are frescoes from 1812 depicting the Nativity and some gruesome scenes from Revelation. ➋ Str Antim 29 Ⓦ www.cimec.ro Ⓛ Dawn–dusk daily

Mănastirea Mihai Vodă (Mihai Vodă Monastery)

This neo-Byzantine-style monastery, which dates from 1601, was moved – on rails – 285 m (935 ft) west in 1985 to make way for the apartment blocks that now hide it from view. It suffered structural damage as a result, and its interior frescoes were badly cracked. Restoration continues and the place occasionally closes without warning. ➋ Str Sapienței 2 Ⓛ 08.00–20.00 daily

Mănastirea Radu Vodă (Radu Vodă Monastery)

Though well hidden behind Piața Unirii's apartment blocks, it is worth hunting this monastery down, if only for the tranquillity of its gardens and grounds. The monastery church dates from 1613 and is a smaller copy of the Curtea de Argeș at Pitești. It was extensively rebuilt and restored in the 19th century, when Gheorghe Tattarescu added the divine frescoes. ➋ Str Radu Vodă 24A Ⓛ Dawn–dusk daily

Palatul Patriarhal (Patriarchal Palace)

This building has been the spiritual heart of the Romanian Orthodox Church since it was first built in the late 17th century

(most of the current complex dates from the early 20th century).
It remains the home of the head of the church, Patriarch Teoctist,
and its gorgeous little church is open only for services (daily
at around 11.00 and 17.00) and on certain saints' days. You
can, however, freely admire the exterior and the sublime
bell tower (from 1698) at the entrance to the complex.
ⓐ Str Dealul Mitropoliei

Piața & Bulevardul Unirii

No post-war city in Europe changed as much as southern
Bucharest did from 1984 to 1989. It is a chilling experience
to compare a map of Bucharest from the early 1980s with one
from today. The longest, widest street in the city, Bulevardul Unirii,
did not exist, neither did most of Piața Unirii, Calea 13 Septembrie
or Bulevardul Libertății, the streets which run in front of and
alongside the Casa Poporului. Instead, a maze of narrow streets
lined with charming *fin-de-siècle* houses filled the space. The
entire district was razed in 1984 to make way for a new Civic
Centre, the design of which was allegedly based on that of the
North Korean capital, Pyongyang.

The idea of building the Civic Centre, with the Casa Poporului as
its central point, was to create a city within a city, one in which all
of the organs of the communist state could be housed, along with
the functionaries needed to run them. The apartments that line
Bulevardul Unirii were not built for the people whose houses were
knocked down to make way for them; they were instead given tiny,
unheated apartments in the far northwest of Bucharest. Only the
very cream of communist society was to live in the Civic Centre, in
isolation from the miserable souls whose lives they ruined.

Piața Universității

For history fans Piața Universității is the most important place in Bucharest. Though Romania's revolution began elsewhere (at Piața Revoluției), it was here that the back of the communist regime was broken, on the night of 21 December 1989. In the traffic island in the middle of the square crosses commemorate those who died here, including Mihai Gatlan, Bucharest's first revolutionary victim, who was killed at 17.30 on 21 December. The square was also the scene of the Mineriada (Miners' Riot) of June 1990, when miners from the Jiu Valley were brought in by then President Ion Iliescu to put down a student protest against his regime. More than a hundred were killed over two days. More recently the square has been the scene of happier events; it is where the city's residents come to celebrate important victories in sport, stopping traffic as they do so.

The pleasant fountains in Piața Unirii

Besides the InterContinental and the National Theatre, the square's other landmark is the eponymous University (Universitatea). The main building (whose neoclassical façade is actually on Bulevardul Regina Elisabeta) was constructed in 1857. Some impressive statues that stood across the road from the university have been temporarily relocated to Izvor Park while an underground car park is constructed.

CULTURE

Muzeul de Istorie al Evreilor din România (Jewish History Museum)

Housed in a former synagogue dating from 1850, this museum tells the story of Romania's once large Jewish community (which numbered 700,000 before World War II) as well as outlining the horrific events that culminated in the murder of more than half of them during the Holocaust. ⓐ Str Mamulari 3 ⓣ 021 311 08 70 ⓛ 09.00–14.00 Mon–Thur, 09.00–12.00 Fri, 09.00–13.00 Sat, closed Sun

Muzeul Naţional de Istorie al României (National History Museum)

Romania's National History Museum is housed inside a wonderful neoclassical building constructed in 1894–6 and originally used as the headquarters of the Romanian Post Office. Its exhibitions include a full-scale replica of Trajan's Column. ⓐ Calea Victoriei 12 ⓣ 021 315 82 07 ⓦ www.mnir.ro ⓛ 10.00–18.00 Wed–Sun (summer); 09.00–17.00 Wed–Sun (winter); closed Mon & Tues ⓘ Admission charge

Teatru Național (National Theatre)

This is in fact two buildings in one. The original National Theatre was built in 1967–70 and was styled as a modernist tribute to the steep-roofed wooden churches of Maramureș, a region in the far north of Romania. When Elena Ceaușescu became directly responsible for the Ministry of Culture in the late 1970s, however, she ordered the building to be covered with the (not unappealing) neoclassical casing we see today. Inside the main lobby you can see how the newer structure was placed over the old. See also page 87. ⓐ Piața 21 Decembrie 1989

RETAIL THERAPY

Hanul cu Tei This is a collective of artisans who all exhibit their wares in the courtyard of a former inn. There are a dozen shops in all, and you can find lace, porcelain, pottery and paintings. ⓐ Str Lipscani 63–65 ⓣ 021 313 01 81 ⓛ 09.00–18.00 Mon–Fri, 09.00–14.00 Sat & Sun

Sticerom Like Hanul cu Tei, this is a collective of artisans. Look out for high-quality glass (made on the premises), including richly colourful glass icons. ⓐ Str Selari 9–11 ⓣ 021 315 96 99 ⓛ 09.30–18.00 Mon–Fri, 09.30–15.00 Sat, closed Sun

Unirea Shopping Center Hundreds of small concessions sell everything imaginable from perfumes to fashion, hi-tech gadgets to hi-fis. ⓐ Piața Unirii 1 ⓣ 021 303 02 08 ⓦ www.unireashop.ro ⓛ 10.00–22.00 daily

TAKING A BREAK

Cafe des Beaux Arts ££ Gallic charm exudes from this understated little place, whose décor reflects the artistic bent of the owners. The service and the coffee both ensure plenty of repeat trade. ⓐ Str Franceză 7 ⓣ 021 310 86 44 ⓛ 14.00–24.00 Tues–Sun, closed Mon

Chocolat ££ ❷ Serving far more than the desserts its name might suggest, Chocolat's extensive menu includes light mains

⬤ Classy Caru cu Bere is a great place to pass an evening

and salads, though those with a sweet tooth won't be disappointed. The jolly rustic theme enhances the cheery feel. Sit at the back for a less smoky eating experience. ⓐ Calea Victoriei 12A ⓣ 021 314 92 45 ⓦ www.chocolat.com.ro ⓛ 09.00–23.00 Mon–Fri, 09.00–last customer Sat & Sun

Charme £££ ❸ The most classy and expensive of the Lipscani cafés, frequented by a somewhat affected crowd. Sexy velvet sofas and great sandwiches. ⓐ Str Smârdan 12 ⓣ 021 311 19 22 ⓦ www.charme.ro ⓛ 09.00–23.00 or 23.30 daily

Festival 39 £££ ❹ Serving coffee and simple food. The tables by the windows – which look out onto Piaţa Unirii – are top see-and-be-seen spots. ⓐ Str Franceză 64 ⓣ 0743 339 909 ⓦ www.festival39.com ⓛ 11.00–01.00 Mon–Fri, 15.00–24.00 Sun

AFTER DARK

RESTAURANTS

St George £ ❺ Bucharest's best Hungarian restaurant. Enjoy fine fresh goose liver and *Debrecener* sausages in a lively dining room setting before washing it all down with one of the five Azsu dessert wines. ⓐ Str Franceză 44 ⓣ 021 317 10 87 ⓦ www.stgeorge.ro ⓛ 11.00–23.00 daily

Caru cu Bere ££ ❻ Housed in a breathtakingly glamorous century-old inn, Caru cu Bere buzzes with atmosphere. In the evenings, live music and dancing jolly things along even more. The food is respectable Romanian fare. ⓐ Str Stavropoleos 3–5

① 021 313 75 60 **Ⓦ** www.carucubere.ro **Ⓛ** 08.00–24.00 Sun–Thur, 08.00–02.00 Fri & Sat

Count Dracula ££ ❼ Good Romanian food given a lively twist by the chap dressed as Dracula who pops out of a coffin and does a tour of the tables two evenings a week. **ⓐ** Splaiul Independenţei Halelor 8A **①** 021 312 13 53 **Ⓦ** www.count-dracula.ro **Ⓛ** 15.00–01.00 daily

BARS & CLUBS

Club A The students' favourite. Cheap drinks, music from all genres and all eras, and a no-hassle atmosphere make this just about the best place to be in Bucharest of a night. **ⓐ** Str Blanări 14 **①** 021 313 55 92 **Ⓛ** 12.00–05.00 Sun–Fri, 21.00–05.00 Sat

Expirat/Other Side Club Two venues in one: Expirat is a mainstream club playing standard European club music for a younger crowd, while next door Other Side Club plays more experimental and offbeat sounds for a slightly cooler, more knowing and simply older crowd. **ⓐ** Str Ion Brezoianu 4 **①** 073 397 47 28 **Ⓦ** www.expirat.org **Ⓛ** Hours vary, so phone ahead or check on the website, most days 20.00–last customer

Harp Though Bucharest has many more exciting venues, if you're hankering after the homely, this does-exactly-what-it-says-on-the-tin Irish pub is a decent enough option. **ⓐ** Str Bibescu Vodă 1 **①** 021 335 65 08 **Ⓛ** 09.00–02.00 daily **❶** Reservations are essential at weekends

Mojo Split into three different levels, this energetic new hotspot has live bands and DJs in the basement, British boozer-style drinking on the ground floor and karaoke and chill-out space upstairs. It all adds up to a refreshingly unpretentious night out. ⓐ Str Gabroveni 14 ⓣ 0760 263 496 ⓦ www.mojomusic.ro ⓛ 13.00–late daily

Whispers Serving the best English breakfast in Bucharest, this pub and grill is a favourite with the expat community that throngs here to watch English football, cricket and rugby on the large screens. ⓐ Str Ion Brezoianu 4 ⓣ 021 314 29 01 ⓦ www.whispers.ro ⓛ 10.00–01.00 Mon–Fri, 12.00–01.00 Sat & Sun

ARTS VENUES

Opera Naţională Bucureşti The Romanian National Opera sticks to a simple and well-known repertoire. While a lack of funding means sets are less than spectacular, the standard of performers is high. All performances except Sunday matinees begin at 18.30. ⓐ B-dul Mihail Kogălniceanu 70–72 ⓣ 021 314 69 80 ⓦ www.operanb.ro ⓛ Box office: 10.00–12.00 daily

Teatru Naţional There is unlikely to be that much on at the National Theatre to interest non-Romanian speakers, though sometimes the venue is used for major concerts and shows. Check listings for details. ⓐ Piaţa 21 Decembrie 1989 ⓣ 021 314 71 71 ⓦ www.tnb.ro ⓛ Box office: 10.00–16.00 Mon, 10.00–19.00 Tues–Sun

Northern Bucharest

The leafy northern part of Bucharest is where the city's rich or well-connected live, and where the whole city comes to play in Herăstrău, the largest park in the city. Characterised by wide boulevards and set-piece buildings, some of the distances between sights in this part of Bucharest are long, and you may be jumping in and out of taxis some of the time. Fortunately, however, many of the sights in northern Bucharest are half or even a full day's outing in themselves, including the Village Museum, Peasant Museum and Herăstrău Park.

SIGHTS & ATTRACTIONS

Arcul de Triumf

It is likely that you will see Arcul de Triumf for the first time as you drive into the city from the airport. Slightly smaller than its more famous namesake in Paris, the Arc was built in 1930 to honour those killed in World War I; it replaced a 1919 wooden structure. The viewing gallery at the top is currently closed to the public. ❸ Piața Arcul de Triumf

Casa Scanteii/Casa Presei Libere

At the head of Şos Kiseleff, this monolithic building is often mistaken by first-time visitors for the Casa Poporului. This is an earlier construction, the first major socialist building project to be completed (in 1956, mainly by forced labourers), and is a smaller replica of the Palace of Science and Culture in Warsaw, Poland. Designed by local architect Horia Maicu, it was built to house all of the communist-era newspapers, as well as the state press agency. It still serves much the same purpose, though the newspapers inside are all now in private hands. You can wander in to admire the marble entrance hall in the day, but everywhere else is closed. ⓐ Piața Presei Libere 1

Herăstrău Park

Set over 187 hectares (462 acres), this wonderful park is where much of the city comes to spend warm weekend afternoons.

🔺 *Arcul de Triumf commemorates casualties of World War I*

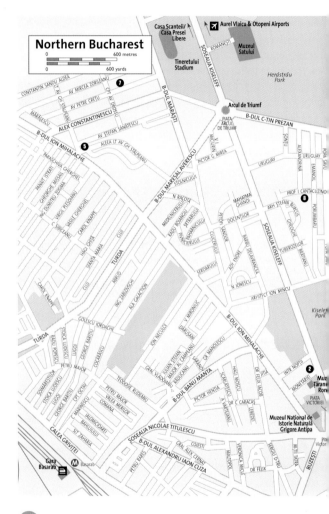

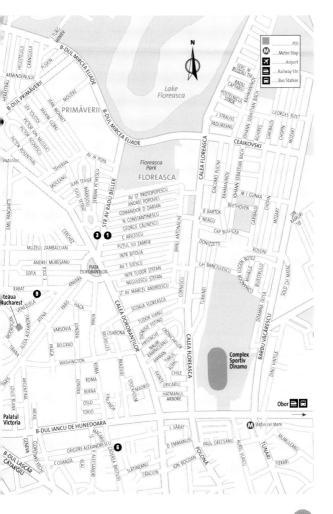

It sits around a vast lake and much of it has been restored to pristine condition. It boasts a number of alleys and paths, all lined with a wide variety of native Romanian flowers, as well as numerous spots for picnic lunches. There are pleasure-boat rides around the lake during the summer, and a couple of launches for sailing boats, which can be hired. For the less nautically experienced, pedalo boats are popular. On the northern shore is a raft of terraces, a go-cart track and a small amusement park with old-fashioned rollercoasters, dodgems and trampolines. The main entrance, which was recently decorated with a large bronze statue of the great French general, is from Piața Charles de Gaulle. ⓐ Șos Kiseleff/Piața Charles de Gaulle 🕐 24 hrs daily

Piața Victoriei

Only slightly smaller than Piața Unirii, Piața Victoriei is another of Bucharest's squares ruined by traffic. Its saving grace is the sleek government building on the eastern side with a neoclassical façade, originally the home of the Foreign Ministry. The southern side is all communist blocks, while the northern is home to Bucharest's tallest skyscraper, the 120 m (394 ft) Europa House (the HQ of a bank and closed to the public). The square is completed by three museums: the Grigore Antipa Museum of Natural History, a stunning place both inside and out; the Peasant Museum, the city's finest; and the Geology Museum, a dull collection of rocks.

Șoseaua Kiseleff

Named after a popular Russian general who did much for the city during his station here in the mid-19th century, Kiseleff (Kiselev on older maps) is Bucharest's Park Lane. Gorgeous villas stand in detached isolation amidst sumptuous grounds. Most are too big to run as private residences, and many have been converted into banking headquarters, foreign embassies or car showrooms. A walk along this street is a stark reminder of how rich the Bucharest bourgeoisie once was, and a great introduction to the idiosyncrasies of Romanian architecture. The small park at the southern end has a good children's playground.

CULTURE

Muzeul Național de Istorie Naturală Grigore Antipa (Grigore Antipa Museum of Natural History)

The renovated exterior of this cracking museum is as much an attraction as the exhibitions inside. There are displays of fossils and long-extinct animals, including a woolly mammoth, as well as the only complete dinosaur skeleton in the country. In the basement there is a fantastic display of sea life, and everything is brilliantly presented with Romanian and English captions. There is also an ever-increasing number of interactive displays, and it is a great place to bring children. Beware though; there is also a display of live reptiles complete with lizards, snakes and baby alligators. ② Șos Kiseleff 1 ① 021 312 88 26 ⓦ www.antipa.ro ① Closed for renovation. Check the website for the latest news about reopening

Muzeul Satului (Village Museum)

King Carol II founded this open-air museum in 1936 so that Bucharest's urbanites could see how the peasantry lived. He had

◔ *The fascinating open-air Village Museum*

more than 60 houses, farmsteads, stables, windmills, watermills and even a church brought here from all of Romania's regions. Every exhibit is well labelled, many with recordings (in English and Romanian) explaining the history of the house and its region. Most people flock first to the extraordinary church of Maramureș, an enormous wooden building from the early 18th century, whose faded but visible frescoes whet the appetite for a visit to the remote Maramureș region itself, where every village has at least one such church. The museum has a great gift shop, and a stall outside sells sweet Romanian delicacies. ⓐ Șos Kiseleff 28–30 ⓣ 021 317 91 10 ⓦ www.muzeul-satului.ro ⓛ 09.00–19.00 Tues–Sun, 09.00–17.00 Mon ⓘ Open all year round but some houses and buildings close during winter. ⓘ Admission charge

Muzeul Țăranului Român (Peasant Museum)

Bucharest's best museum. You can spend the best part of a day trawling around the thousands upon thousands of exhibits that display the ingenuity, craft and skill of the Romanian peasant. Enjoy vivid descriptions of country life, traditions and the histories of the particular group of Romanians who executed the work. Most popular are the intricately painted Easter eggs Romanians used to give each other at Easter (but now seldom do); you can buy replicas in the superb gift shop. Look out, too, for the religious art, from carved icons to sacred texts woven into fabric, as well as the vast room presenting traditional costumes from Romania's regions. In the basement is an exhibition about communism – a vast collection of portraits, busts, flags, banners, emblems and newspaper articles from the darkest era of Romania's recent past. It is the only place in the city you will still find a portrait of Nicolae Ceaușescu. ⓐ Șos Kiseleff 3 ⓣ 021 317 96 60 ⓦ www.muzeultaranuluiroman.ro ⓛ 10.00–18.00 Tues–Sun, closed Mon ⓘ Admission charge

RETAIL THERAPY

Mario Plaza In wealthy Dorobanti this exclusive shopping mall is the well-located home of a small number of high-end fashion

⬥ Head to the Peasant Museum for authentic Romanian souvenirs

shops for men, women and children, perfumeries, interior design outlets, a good bookshop and a trendy café. ⓐ Calea Dorobanților 172 ⓣ 021 230 47 71 ⓦ www.marioplaza.eu ⓛ 10.00–21.00 Mon–Sat, 10.00–14.00 Sun

Muzeul Satului (Village Museum) A smaller version of the Peasant Museum shop (see below), with emphasis placed on religious items. ⓐ Șos Kiseleff 28–30 ⓣ 021 317 91 10 ⓦ www.muzeul-satului.ro ⓛ See page 95

Muzeul Țăranului Român (Peasant Museum) If you do not find a souvenir here, then you are really in trouble. If it is made in Romania and involves skill and craft, you will find it in this shop, from full national costume to charming wooden carved figures. Prices are not cheap but everyone will find something they can afford. ⓐ Șos Kiseleff 3 ⓣ 021 317 96 60 ⓛ See page 96

TAKING A BREAK

When it comes to cafés, one street in northern Bucharest is head and shoulders above all others: Strada Av Radu Beller, where it meets Piața Dorobanților. It is lined with coffee houses and is the closest thing this part of town gets to a 'strip'.

La Belle Epoque ££ ❶ A Belgian beer café with only the finest Belgian beers, from conventional Stella Artois and Hoegaarden to less well-known Trappist beers such as Chimay. The good food menu is well priced. ⓐ Str Av Radu Beller 6 ⓣ 021 230 07 70 ⓦ www.labelleepoque.ro ⓛ 08.00–24.00 daily

Casa Doina ££ ② This is one of the oldest restaurants in the city, designed for the Romanian Pavilion at the 1904 World Fair. It didn't make the fair, so was instead erected in the heart of Bucharest's smartest suburb. Great Romanian and international dishes. During the day it is a charming place for a good-value lunch. ⓐ Şos Kiseleff 4 ① 021 222 67 17 ⓦ www.casadoina.ro ⓛ 12.00–01.00 daily

Chocolat ££ ③ Though the name might suggest it's just a patisserie, this cosy eatery serves a great range of light meals alongside indulgent desserts. Part of a small chain, there's another outlet on Calea Victoriei in the old town (see page 84). A similar French-style option is Paul, just a few doors down. ⓐ Str Av Radu Beller 13 ① 021 230 23 83 ⓦ www.chocolat.com.ro ⓛ 09.00–23.00 Mon–Fri, 09.00–last customer Sat & Sun

City Grill ££ ④ It's hard to go wrong at this fantastic Romanian café and restaurant. There are local treats on the menu, as well as a great selection of local beers. Despite the upmarket location, prices are relatively good value. ⓐ B-dul Primăverii 3 ① 021 233 98 18 ⓛ 10.00–02.00 daily

AFTER DARK

RESTAURANTS
Barka Saffron £–££ ⑤ It may not generate as much excitement as it did back in the day when Barka was a pioneer on the gastronomic scene, but the Indian and Indonesian mix still has its fans. ⓐ Av Stefan Sănătescu 1 ① 021 224 10 04 ⓛ 12.00–23.30 Mon–Fri, 10.00–23.30 Sat & Sun

La Bastille ££ ❻ Charming French restaurant where food is treated as art and the staff are efficient and knowledgeable. Prices are remarkably good. Try to get a table in the upstairs dining room. ⓐ Str Căderea Bastiliei 72B ❶ 021 310 73 59 ⓦ www.labastille.ro ⓛ 12.00–24.00 daily

Thai Moods ££ ❼ Authentic, tasty Thai food. Best during the summer, when the big garden at the back is open. At other times make a reservation, as there are just a few tables inside. ⓐ Str Av Petre Crețu 63 ❶ 021 224 68 51 ⓦ www.thaimoods.ro ⓛ 17.00–24.00 Tues–Sat, closed Sun & Mon

Arcade £££ ❽ A luxurious place with fine food. The vaguely Italian menu has some modern European touches. ⓐ Str Prof I Cantacuzino 8 ❶ 021 260 29 60 ⓦ www.restaurantarcade.ro ⓛ 12.00–24.00 daily

Uptown £££ ❾ What brings people to this place is the terrace, covered by a heated canopy that means you can sit outside in December. The food is inventive if a little overpriced and the service is variable, but the home-made butter is the best around. ⓐ Str Rabat 2 ❶ 021 231 40 77 ⓦ www.uptown.ro ⓛ 12.00–24.00 daily

BARS & CLUBS
Bamboo A flashy nightspot on Lake Tei. It is best in summer when the trendy crowd spills out onto the terrace. Expect a more mainstream disco soundtrack than elsewhere. ⓐ Str Tuzla 50 ⓦ www.bambooclub.ro ⓛ 22.00–late Thur–Sun, closed Mon–Wed

Dubliner The original expat pub, the Dubliner offers live televised British sports, steak and kidney pie, the city's best jukebox and a covered terrace which is great in winter. Şos N Titulescu 18 021 222 94 73 09.00–02.00 daily

Kristal Glam Club Kristal almost single-handedly turned the Romanian capital into a decent club venue. Expect the best local and international DJs and expensive drinks. Sitting at a table costs €100, so come prepared to dance. Str J S Bach 2 021 231 21 36 or 0722 795 184 www.clubkristal.ro from 23.00 daily

Studio Martin Expect only the biggest names in club music from around the world. Entrance ticket costs vary with the stock value of the DJ in question. B-dul Iancu de Hunedoara 41 0722 399 228 www.studiomartin.ro 22.00–05.00 Fri & Sat, closed Sun–Thur

White Horse A lively pub and restaurant in the Dorobanti area of the city. Popular with locals and expats, it can get very lively on weekend evenings. Str George Călinescu 4A 021 231 27 95 www.whitehorse.ro restaurant 12.00–23.00, pub 11.00–last customer daily

 The stunning Transylvanian Alps, north of Bucharest

OUT OF TOWN
trips

Around Bucharest: lakes, palaces & monasteries

Bucharest stands somewhat isolated on the plain of Wallachia, surrounded in the main by small villages with no interest for the visitor. There are some worthwhile excursions, however, mainly to the medieval monasteries built to give thanks for victory in battle, and the 18th-century palaces that were built to house the city's rich in splendid isolation. There are also lakes and forests, nature reserves and Eastern Europe's largest film studio.

GETTING THERE

There are trains from Gara de Nord during summer weekends to Mogoșoaia and Snagov, though they are of the dirty, slow type and are not recommended. The stations are also some distance from the attractions they serve. It is a better idea to take the ⓝ bus: 444 from Piața Presei Libere for Snagov, and bus 460 from Laromet for Mogoșoaia and Buftea. There is no public transport to Caldarușani. Bucharest taxis will take you to all of the places featured here, though note that tariffs double once you leave the city limits, and rare is the taxi driver who will drive out here to bring you home at the end of the day. Indeed, the only way to see all of these sights and attractions is with your own car (see details of car hire on page 56). It takes around 30 minutes by car to get to all of these places and double that by public transport.

SIGHTS & ATTRACTIONS

Lacul Snagov (Lake Snagov)

The largest of the lakes that surround Bucharest, Snagov, 37 km (23 miles) north of the city, has a long history as a summer recreational retreat for Bucharest's block-bound residents. More recently it has become their home; more than 1,200 villas now surround all sides of the lake. Many people still come here for the day, however, to fish, barbecue, swim, hire rowing boats or cycle in the surrounding forests. For the active visitor, a day here can be rewarding. You can paddle kayaks (with or without an instructor), take a speedboat ride, play tennis or even learn how to scuba dive. All of these activities take place at Snagov Beach (Snagov Plaja) on the southern side of the lake. Speedboat trips have to be arranged in advance with **Snagov Tur** in Bucharest (**❶** 021 323 99 05 **Ⓦ** www.snagov.ro). South of the lake is a small nature reserve, Snagov Rezervat, whose flora and fauna, including deer, pheasants and owls, are protected. A number of bird-watching posts have been set up around the reserve. **ⓐ** Complex Turistic Snagov, Sat Snagov, Comuna Snagov **❶** 021 323 99 05

Mănastirea Caldaruşani (Caldaruşani Monastery)

Situated on a peninsula 6 km (3¹/₂ miles) southeast of Lake Snagov, the monastery of Caldaruşani was built in 1637 by Matei Basarab, then ruler of Wallachia, to give thanks for victory over Moldavian Prince Vasile Lupu in the Battle of Teleajen. The structure of the three-towered monastery church remains, but the frescoes inside have faded badly, though those featuring Basarab and his wife

remain miraculously intact. The rest of the monastery complex
dates from 1775–8, when it was expanded by Ghenadie Petrescu,
patriarch of the Romanian Orthodox Church. In the monastery's
museum is a fine collection of religious art, including icons painted
by the Romanian maestro Nicolae Grigorescu. ⓐ Mănastirea
Caldaruşani, Sat Lipia, Comuna Snagov ⓦ www.manastirea-
caldarusani.go.ro ⓛ 08.00–18.00 daily

Mănastirea Snagov (Snagov Monastery)

Snagov's main attraction for visitors is the monastery on a tiny
island in the middle of the lake, which reputedly contains the

headless body of Vlad III Țepeș, the inspiration behind the Dracula myth. The monastery was founded in 1408 by Mircea cel Batran (Mircea the Old), though rebuilt from 1512 to 1521 during the reign of Neagoe Basarab, and modelled on the church of Mount Athos in Greece. It is Basarab who, alongside his wife, appears in the votive frescoes inside the church. On the opposite wall are rich paintings of another Wallachian ruler, Mircea Ciobanul (Mircea the Shepherd), and the whole ensemble represents the largest collection of medieval paintings in southern Romania. The tomb

🔻 *Caldaruşani Monastery, southeast of Lake Snagov*

of Vlad III Țepeș is found underneath the church, marked only by a painting of Vlad. The church and tower in front of it are all that remain of the original monastery, the other buildings on the island having been added over the following centuries. The only way to get to the island is from the south side of the lake in a self-rowed hired boat from the Complex Astoria Turistic Snagov. ➊ Sat Siliștea Snagovului, Comuna Snagov ➍ Dawn–dusk daily

Media Pro Film Studios
Once the state-run film studio that created epics featuring Romanians doing battle with the Turks, Romans and Hungarians, the Buftea studios were acquired by the team

DRACULA LAND

Romania has long hoped to cash in on the Dracula myth, and for a decade was toying with the idea of setting up a Dracula theme park. The first attempt was in the Transylvanian town of Sighișoara, but local opposition and embezzlement of funds saw the project get no further than the planning stage. A subsequent proposal for 'Dracula Land,' centred on Lake Snagov, where the local council and population seemed more open to the idea. Though UNESCO opposition and financial limitations appear to have staked the idea for now, it remains to be seen whether it will rise from the dead when the Romanian economy picks up.

⬤ *The splendid architecture of Mogoşoaia Palace*

behind Pro TV, Romania's leading TV station, and quickly became world-renowned. A number of major, award-winning movies have been filmed here, as well as the two-part drama, *Sex Traffic*, the winner of eight BAFTAs and numerous other awards in 2005. The studios are vast and the management has recently begun opening them up to visitors, eager to show what the Romanian film industry is capable of. What's more, tours are free; you just need to book a day or two in advance. ⓐ Str Studioului 1, Buftea ⓣ 031 825 13 03 ⓦ www.mediaprostudios.com

Palatul Mogoșoaia (Mogoșoaia Palace)

Some 14 km (8½ miles) north of the capital, Mogoșoaia is today a growing, middle-class suburb of Bucharest. The great Renaissance man Constantin Brâncoveanu – prince, politician and the dominant force in late 17th-century Wallachia – built himself a palace here in 1680. In 1688 Brâncoveanu, by then Prince of Wallachia, moved his entire court here, and a village grew around the palace, including a tiny but wonderful church which is usually the first thing visitors see. The six short columns that support the church's portico were much copied by 18th- and 19th-century Romanian architects, giving rise to a style that became known as Brâncovenesque. Brâncoveanu and his entire family are superbly depicted on the church's interior walls.

The main attraction is of course the palace itself, a vast and richly decorated building surrounded by well-kept grounds ideal for picnics. Much of the furniture is original, as is the décor, including more portraits of Brâncoveanu and his family. ⓐ Valea Parcului 1, Comuna Mogoșoaia ⓣ 021 312 88 94 ⓛ 10.00–17.00 Tues–Fri, 10.00–18.00 Sat & Sun, closed Mon

RETAIL THERAPY

Baneasa Shopping City On the main road halfway between Bucharest's two airports, you can take care of any shopping needs you may have here. Open daily from 10.00 to 22.00, it is big enough to fit every other Bucharest shopping centre inside in some comfort, and features thousands of shops, many of which – such as Next, Oviesse, Gas and Replay – opened their Romanian outlets here. Add in a huge IKEA next door, as well as a Carrefour hypermarket, and you have at least a day of retail action. ⓦ www.baneasashoppingcity.ro ⓛ shops 10.00–22.00, restaurants 10.00–23.00 daily

TAKING A BREAK

Casa Romaneasca ££ Large, tasty portions of excellent Romanian dishes, including the best *mici* (small tangy meatballs, a speciality of Wallachia) you'll ever taste. Service can be a bit slow, however. ⓐ Calea Bucureştilor 258, Călimăneşti ⓣ 025 075 17 07 ⓦ www.casa-romaneasca.ro ⓛ 10.00–24.00 daily

Starbucks ££ Romania gets a taste of America at what may sound like a familiar chain brand to you but is, in the local context, a phenomenon beamed in from another planet. Choose from the usual endless list of coffees, as well as a great selection of sandwiches, cakes and muffins. The chain's no-smoking policy doesn't go down well with locals but visitors tend to approve. ⓐ Baneasa Shopping City, Ground Floor, Şos Bucureşti-Ploiesti 42D ⓛ 10.00–23.00 daily

AFTER DARK

Mogoşoaia Palace Restaurant ££ Inside one of the largest and grandest rooms of the palace, this superb restaurant serves outstanding traditional Romanian food at thoroughly decent prices. ❸ Valea Parcului 1, Comuna Mogoşoaia ❶ 021 312 88 94 ❶ 12.00–22.00 Tues–Sun, closed Mon ❶ Booked out for weddings almost every weekend in summer

Vânatorul ££ 'The Hunter' unsurprisingly serves game dishes of all kinds in a superb setting on the edge of Snagov Forest. More standard Romanian specialities are also found on the menu, and a live Roma band knocks out enjoyable but loud music most summer evenings. ❸ Sat Snagov, Comuna Snagov ❶ 0722 861 471 ❶ 11.30–23.00 daily

Al Casolare £££ Never before has the phrase 'just like Mother cooks at home' been more appropriate. Why? Because this restaurant is someone's home and the chef is someone's mother (the waiter's). The food is top-class Italian, served in enormous portions. ❸ Şos Bucureşti-Targoviste Km 45, Comuna Mogoşoaia ❶ 021 351 41 86 ⓦ www.alcasolare.ro ❶ 18.00–24.00 Tues–Fri, 12.00–03.00 Sat & Sun, closed Mon ❶ Reservations compulsory

ACCOMMODATION

Complex Astoria Snagov £ On the southern edge of Lake Snagov, there's a choice of two- or three-star accommodation in a motel, in small wooden villas or in bungalows. On-site tennis courts and children's playground are included. ⓐ Sat Snagov, Comuna Snagov ① 021 314 83 20 or 021 794 04 60

Complex Confort Rin £ Budget choice close to the main airport, Otopeni, with a poor location but large rooms in two categories. Mostly used by provincial Romanians who have to catch early flights. ⓐ Calea Bucureștilor 255 ① 021 350 41 10 ⓦ www.rinhotels.ro

Motanul Galanton £ Small but classy little *pension* in Ghermanești. Ten rooms, all with great beds and bathrooms, with larger rooms available for families. Small outdoor swimming pool, gym, sauna and great breakfast included. ⓐ Șos Ghermanești 18, Sat Ghermanești ① 021 351 06 39 or 0722 222 353 ⓦ www.motanulgalanton.ro

Angelo Airport Hotel ££ Opposite the entrance to Bucharest's Otopeni airport, this hotel is a smart place with a host of luxury extras. A good location if you're planning to explore the surrounding monasteries by car. Transfers to and from terminals and a great breakfast are included in the price. ⓐ Calea Bucureștilor 283 ① 021 203 65 00 ⓦ www.angelo-bucharest.com

Sinaia

Sinaia is a small town 99 km (61½ miles) north of Bucharest, noted for its outstanding hiking in the Bucegi range during summer months, and some wild and challenging skiing during the winter. The town takes its name from its monastery, founded in 1695 by Romanian nobleman Mihai Cantacuzino after a pilgrimage to Mt Sinai in Egypt. Situated at an altitude of 800 m (2,625 ft), it became a fashionable mountain resort after Carol I built his summer palace here, Peleş, at the end of the 19th century.

GETTING THERE

It takes about two hours to get to Sinaia from the capital, and the best way to do so is by train; fast intercity services from Bucharest to Brasov stop here. Tickets can be bought one hour before departure from Gara de Nord station, or further in advance from the **SNCFR booking office** in the city centre (ⓐ Strada

WHEN TO VISIT

If you can, avoid visiting Sinaia on winter weekends, when the capital's skiers flock here. If you come during the week you will often have the slopes to yourself. Likewise in summer, avoid weekends in August, when once again the hotels and villas are full of Bucharest residents escaping the summer heat.

● *Sinaia is a top skiing destination*

Domnita Anastasia 10–14 ☎ 021 313 26 43 ◷ 07.30–19.30 Mon–Fri, 08.00–12.00 Sat, closed Sun). Sinaia's railway station is at the bottom of the town, and it's a steep climb up to the main street, Bulevardul Carol I. The station is an elegant pile, built to accommodate the Orient Express, which passed through here on its way to Istanbul. Driving here can take a little longer as the road up is narrow and steep in places, with plenty of hairpin bends. If you do choose to drive, follow signs for Ploieşti from the north of the capital, and from there for Brasov. The main Bucharest–Brasov road runs through the middle of the resort.

SIGHTS & ATTRACTIONS

Hiking in the Bucegi

The mountains that overlook Sinaia, the Bucegi, may not be the highest in Europe but they are certainly among the most spectacular. Jagged stone peaks poke into the clouds and a host of natural wonders dot the landscape, from the Sphinx-like rock over at neighbouring Bușteni to the highland Lake Bolboci. The range is criss-crossed with a vast number of hiking trails of all levels. Beginners are best advised to take the cable car up to the top and simply walk down. The plateau at Sinaia Cota 2000, at the top of the cable car, is a great spot for a picnic. Another popular walk for day-trippers is from Sinaia Cota 2000 over to Cabana Ciorcaila and then down to Bușteni via La Scara, a sensational natural stone stairway that passes the equally remarkable Cascada Urlatoarea (Shrieking Waterfall). From Bușteni a taxi or train will take you back to Sinaia. More experienced hikers can use Sinaia as a base to explore much of the mid-Carpathians. There are routes from Sinaia over to Bran, Râșnov and Moeciu de Sus. Cabins dot the mountains and offer food and beds for the night.

Even if you are just setting out for a day trip on one of the well-marked routes, you should always be prepared for bad weather; take warm clothing, water and chocolate. Never set off without a decent map (a good one can be purchased at the cable-car station) and always stick to marked tracks. ❸ Cable car: Str Telefericului ⏱ approximately 08.45–15.45 Dec–Feb; 08.30–16.30 Mar–May; 09.00–17.00 June–Nov daily

◯ *The dramatic scenery of the Bucegi mountains*

◆ *The fairytale-like Peleş Castle*

Castelul Peleş (Peleş Castle)

Set 100 m (328 ft) or so above Sinaia, this magnificent castle is straight out of a fairytale. The first King of Romania, Carol I, visited Sinaia in 1866 to stay at the monastery and fell in love with the place. He bought land here seven years later and had Wilhelm Doderer, a German architect, build this palace as a summer retreat. Work was not finally completed until 1904. The compulsory guided tour takes in all of the more exotic rooms of the palace, decorated by artists from all over Europe. Some rooms are replicas of Turkish and Moorish castle halls, others are decorated in more conventional neo-Renaissance style. In the grounds is the smaller but, for many, more tasteful Pelişor (Little Peleş) castle, built for Carol's heir Ferdinand and his English wife Queen Marie. A separate entrance ticket is needed for this. Tickets for both Pelişor and the main palace tour have to be purchased at the entrance gate to the grounds. ⓐ Str Peleşului 2 ⓣ 0244 31 09 18 ⓦ www.peles.ro ⓛ 09.00–17.00 Tues–Sun, closed Mon (mid-May–mid-Sept); 11.00–17.00 Wed, 09.00–17.00 Thur–Sun, closed Mon & Tues (mid-Sept–mid-May) ⓘ Admission charge

Mănastirea Sinaia (Sinaia Monastery)

The pick of the buildings at the Sinaia Monastery is the tiny, white 1695 monastery church, which boasts some of the oldest frescoes in this part of Romania. The paintings on the portal, depicting the Last Judgement in graphic detail, date back to the church's construction. The gorgeous neoclassical porch that protects the frescoes from the elements was added in the 19th century. Equally striking is the larger and newer of the monastery's churches, the neo-Byzantine red and white building that dominates

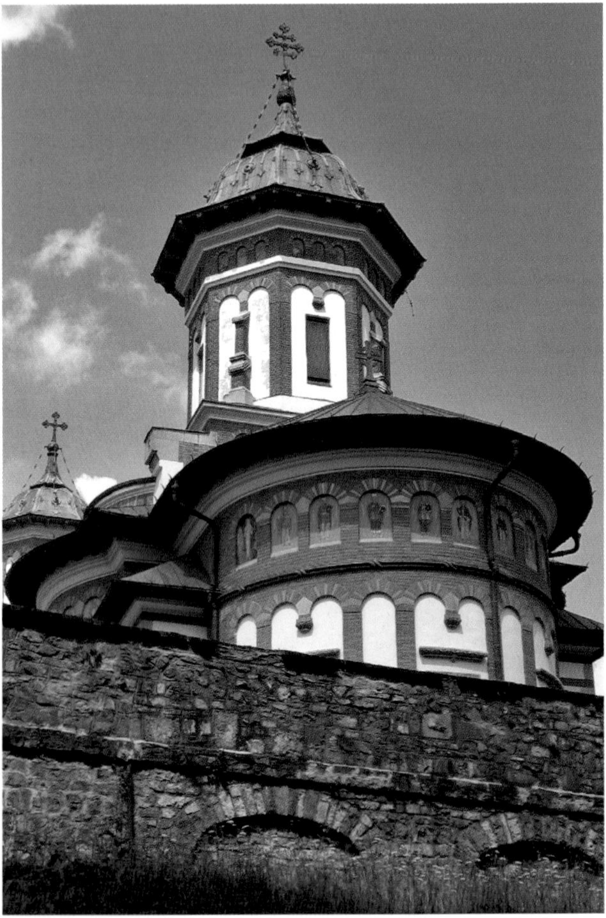

The neo-Byzantine centrepiece of Sinaia Monastery

the centre of the site. Built in 1842, it boasts some superb gold-leaf murals and a wonderful carved oak altar. There is also a museum on site containing hundreds of Orthodox religious relics, from illustrated Slavonic Bibles to liturgical robes. In the Paraclis, a small chapel in the corner of the monastery, are more 300-year-old frescoes. ⓐ Str Mănăstirii ☎ 0244 31 49 17 ⏲ services 08.00–20.00, museum 10.00–16.00 Mon–Sat, closed Sun (summer); in winter museum opened only for organised groups of ten or more ⓘ Admission charge

Skiing

Sinaia is best known internationally for its skiing, which has become far more accessible over the past few years with the opening of a brand new gondola lift to get skiers up to Cota 1400, and a four-man chairlift from there up to the main ski area, the Valea Dorului. Situated at 2,000 m (6,561 ft), the skiing up here is open and cruisy, and is served by two further chairlifts

SKIING PRACTICALITIES

Ski hire can be arranged at any of the main hotels, or at a number of ski-hire shacks at the cable-car station, where lift passes are also sold. Budget 70 lei for a day's ski hire, and 50 lei for a day's lift pass. Sinaia is not geared to beginners, and arranging ski lessons is a little difficult. The ski schools are all based at Cota 1400, and you need to take the cable car up to find an instructor. Negotiate with the instructors directly; 30 lei per hour is a good price.

and three drags. Snow is usually guaranteed right into May. To get to Cota 1400, skiers can take the gondola lift, somewhat awkwardly placed a ten-minute uphill walk from the New Montana Hotel, next to the Taverna Sarbului restaurant. You can avoid this by simply staying at the Hotel Cota 1400 (see page 124).

When the snow is good there are two challenging routes all the way from the top station down to the resort: that's a vertical drop of over 1,000 m (3,280 ft) and a good 15 km (9 miles) of skiing (if the snow is poor you need to take the gondola back down to the resort, so ensure you check the time the last one leaves). Officially the resort has 25 km (15½ miles) of marked pistes; modest by international standards, but far more than any other ski area in Romania. ⓐ Gondola: Str Codrului ⓛ 08.45–16.00 Dec–Feb; 08.30–16.30 Mar–May; 09.00–17.00 June–Nov daily

TAKING A BREAK

Cabana Schiorilor £ You can sit on the terrace here summer or winter. Inexpensive, unfussy Romanian cuisine is served by friendly, happy staff. ⓐ Drumul Cotei 7 ⓣ 0244 31 36 55 ⓦ www.cabana-schiori.ro ⓛ 08.00–22.00 daily

The Office Lounge £££ About as trendy a venue as you are going to find at this altitude. Brilliantly located on the first floor of the International Hotel (see page 124), it has enviable views (from both inside and out) of the resort and the mountains, and serves expensive coffee and cakes to people far too important to ski or hike themselves. ⓐ Str Avram Iancu 1, Hotel International ⓣ 0744 326 653 ⓛ 14.00–04.00 daily

AFTER DARK

Beraria Cerbul ££ This is just how a beer hall should be, with good, cheap beer that's made on the premises and served in huge glasses by buxom waitresses in Saxon garb. Good food too, if slow to arrive. ⓐ B-dul Carol I 19 ① 0244 31 47 24 ① 09.00–23.00 daily

Old Nic Pub ££ Decent pizzas are served at cheap prices in an enormous pub on Sinaia's main street. Service can be terrible and getting a table without a reservation tough during the ski season. Lively later in the evening when it doubles as the resort's main nightspot. ⓐ B-dul Carol 22 ① 0244 31 24 91 ⓦ www.oldnickpub.ro ① 09.00–03.00 daily

Taverna Sarbului £££ The original Taverna Sarbului (there are sister establishments in Bucharest and Brasov) is a joy of meaty treats, including a good selection of game dishes, served in enormous portions at decent prices. Not a place for vegetarians. ⓐ Calea Codrului ① 0244 17 12 00 ⓦ www.tavernasarbului.ro ① 12.00–23.00 daily

ACCOMMODATION

Sinaia £ A basic thee-star package holiday hotel expensively facelifted. Rooms are small but all have balconies with great mountain views, bathrooms and oversized televisions. The hotel has a small indoor, heated swimming pool. ⓐ B-dul Carol I 8 ① 0244 30 29 14 ⓦ www.hotelsinaia.ro

Hotel Cota 1400 ££ If you really like the mountains, or just simply want to make sure that you are first on the ski slopes in the morning, where better to stay than halfway up the cable car? The hotel has large, well-equipped rooms with fantastic views and a restaurant and bar too. @ Drumul Cotei ❶ 0244 31 49 90 ⓦ www.hotel-cota1400.ro

International ££ Sinaia's most luxurious hotel is this renovated 1970s high-rise that sits commandingly at the entrance to the resort. Decent-sized – though a tad overpriced – rooms with enormous baths, efficient staff and great views from even the lower floors. @ Str Avram Iancu 1 ❶ 0244 31 38 51 ⓦ www.international-sinaia.ro

Palace ££ Sinaia's once classy Palace hotel, built in 1911, retains a kind of faded grandeur that sets it apart from the modern giants that dominate the centre of the resort. Rooms are huge if spartan, the restaurant a neoclassical gem, and the park surroundings quiet and relaxed. @ Str Octavian Goga 4 ❶ 0244 31 20 51

New Montana £££ Great breakfast and newly renovated four-star accommodation ideal for the cable car, which is directly behind the hotel. The large swimming pool is open to non-guests. @ B-dul Carol I 24 ❶ 0244 31 27 51 ⓦ www.newmontana.ro ❶ 10.00–22.00 daily ❶ Admission charge

❶ *Hustle and bustle along Piața Unirii*

PRACTICAL
information

Directory

GETTING THERE

You are most likely to arrive in Bucharest by air, with direct flights from the UK, Ireland and various mainland European cities. Arriving by train costs considerably more, and is only really an option if you are visiting Romania on a larger European tour. Driving would take forever and is not really worth considering.

By air

British Airways and Tarom (Romania's national airline) fly direct, once or twice daily from London Heathrow, in around 3 hours and 30 minutes, but their fares are expensive. Wizzair and Blue Air fly direct from Luton with reasonable fares, though as with all budget airlines the sooner in advance you book the cheaper the ticket is. Another option is to travel via another European city. From Ireland, Aer Lingus has direct flights from Dublin.

Aer Lingus ☎ 0871 718 5000 Ⓦ www.aerlingus.com
British Airways ☎ 0844 493 0787 Ⓦ www.ba.com
Tarom ☎ 020 7224 36 93 Ⓦ www.tarom.ro
Wizzair Ⓦ www.wizzair.com

Many people are aware that air travel emits CO_2, which contributes to climate change. You may be interested in the possibility of lessening the environmental impact of your flight through the charity **Climate Care** (Ⓦ www.jpmorganclimatecare. com), which offsets your CO_2 by funding environmental projects around the world.

By rail

At the time of writing it is not possible to buy a through ticket from London or Dublin to Bucharest. The closest you can get is a ticket to Budapest, from where there is a choice of four daily trains to Bucharest (taking from 12 to 15 hours). It takes around 24 hours to get to Budapest from London.

Rail Europe ⓦ www.raileurope.co.uk

The Man in Seat 61 ⓦ www.seat61.com

Thomas Cook European Rail Timetable ☎ 01733 416477 (UK), 1800 322 3834 (US) ⓦ www.thomascookpublishing.com

ENTRY FORMALITIES

Citizens from other European Union countries may enter Romania visa-free with valid picture ID and stay for as long as

◗ *Gara de Nord, Bucharest's main rail station*

they please. Visitors from the US, Australia, New Zealand and Canada can all enter without a visa if their stay does not exceed 90 days. Romanian legislation requires you to have some form of identification on you at all times (though in practice this is seldom checked). A copy of your passport will suffice.

While Romania imposes no limits on goods imported from or exported to the rest of the EU, your home country may impose its own limits on the amount of cigarettes and alcohol you may bring home.

MONEY

The Romanian currency is the leu (plural lei). It is usually written in full, though is sometimes referred to by the acronym RON. One leu is equal to 100 bani. The denominations for notes are 1, 5, 10, 50, 100 and (more rarely) 200 and 500; there are coins in denominations of 50, 10, 5 and 1 bani. Many shops and stores (especially electrical shops) will list prices in lei and euros, but note that euros are not legal tender.

It is all but impossible to obtain Romanian currency outside the country, but there is no need to do so as there are ATMs at all of the country's arrival points, and in thousands of locations all over the country. ATMs accept Visa and MasterCard and are the best places to get your hands on lei. Avoid using bureaux de change as they offer poor rates of exchange. If you do find that you have to change cash, do it inside a bank. Traveller's cheques are met with derision everywhere in Bucharest and are notoriously difficult to get rid of. You will find it difficult to exchange lei outside of Romania, so try not to withdraw too much at any one time.

OUT WITH THE OLD …

The old Romanian leu was replaced with today's currency (the new leu, or RON) in 2005, with four zeros (a result of rampant inflation in the past) getting lopped off. You're very unlikely to encounter an old note – if you do, exchange it in a bank. However, the change has not yet been fully assimilated into Romanians' parlance. If, for example, you're told that a restaurant bill comes to a million lei, do not think you've ordered a €230,000 meal! This is simply how some people refer to 100 lei.

HEALTH, SAFETY & CRIME

Tap water is perfectly safe to drink but given the low price of the bottled variety, nobody actually does. For any minor disorders any pharmacy (*farmacie*) will be able to help; you can buy far more drugs over the counter in Romania than you can at home. Most pharmacies have English-speaking staff, but few are open 24 hours; exceptions include some outlets of HelpNet and Senisblu (see Emergencies, page 136). If you need serious medical attention head for a private medical clinic, such as one of those listed in Emergencies.

Bucharest is a remarkably safe city, and there is virtually no violent crime. Petty crime is a problem, however, so be extra careful when travelling on buses and trams, where pickpocketing is rife, and don't flash your wallet around.

The biggest safety issue you are likely to have to deal with in Bucharest is the city's 100,000-strong stray dog population. Though mostly harmless, in 2006 one such dog attacked and

TRAVEL INSURANCE

It is important to take out adequate personal travel insurance covering medical expenses, theft, loss, repatriation, personal liability and cancellation. EU citizens with a **European Health Insurance Card** (EHIC – apply online at Ⓦ www.ehic.org.uk) will enjoy some free or reduced healthcare, but are advised to have private medical insurance as well. If you are travelling in your own vehicle, make sure you have the appropriate insurance, and remember to pack the insurance documents and your driving licence. You will need to make a police report for non-medical claims and keep any receipts for medical treatment. Consider keeping a copy of your policy and emergency contact numbers in your email account.

killed a Japanese businessman. About 50 people a day are bitten (not fatally) by dogs, but most of the city's population refuse to allow a cull. If you are bitten, get to hospital immediately to have the wound cleaned and get an anti-rabies injection. Though strays are seen more often in the suburbs than in the very heart of the city, you should prepare yourself for at least one encounter with barking dogs. Stay calm, carry on walking and, whatever you do, do not run!

OPENING HOURS

Opening hours of museums are generally 10.00–17.00, and almost all are closed on Mondays. Less well-frequented museums may close early or over lunchtime without warning. Churches are usually open from dawn to dusk. Banking hours are 09.00–17.00 Monday to Friday, (some close early on Friday), closed Saturday and Sunday. General shopping hours are 09.30–19.00, though these are extending, often to 21.00. Most shops – except big malls and shopping centres – close early on Saturdays, and do not open on Sundays. The small kiosks that litter the city centre to sell cigarettes, drinks and snacks generally stay open 24 hours.

TOILETS

Public toilet provision in Bucharest has been improving gradually. Parks now typically have portable loos, which are bearable and sometimes even have loo paper (if not running water for hand-washing). Shopping malls and stations have bathrooms, but don't expect too much. Even in swanky cinemas and restaurants, toilets are often poorly tended. If you want to nip in to a restaurant or café, it's best to ask; McDonald's toilets have door codes so you'll need to buy something. Hotel staff are unlikely to challenge a foreigner striding towards the bathroom, especially in five-star places, which have fabulous toilets. Outside Bucharest, the standard declines considerably.

CHILDREN

There are few attractions geared towards children. One big exception is the Village Museum (see page 93), which children find great fun, as they can climb in and out of the old wooden houses. The Grigore Antipa Museum of Natural History (see page 93) is also relatively interesting for children. The horse-riding centres such as Hipocan (see page 34) on the outskirts of town will also entertain the children. There are bowling and amusement arcades at most of the city's malls too. If you have cash to splash, you can take the children to Sunday brunch at one of the big hotels (most five-star places do it); kids usually eat for less or free and clowns, carers and DVDs will keep them happy while you enjoy your food and champagne. The parks all have well-equipped children's play areas, though don't expect health and safety standards to match what you are used to at home. A particularly impressive play area is the brand new 'Children's Parliament' in Izvor Park.

The following are a few other genuine children's options that may come to the rescue of desperate parents:

Boom Boom Land A smaller version of Children's Island (see below), in the south of the city, with bouncy castles, slides and the like to keep children entertained. In summer there are outdoor activities too. ⓐ B-dul Tineretului ⓣ 021 317 59 01 ⓛ 10.00–21.00 daily ⓘ Admission charge

Grădina Zoologică (Zoo) Despite some recent improvements it remains a bit of a sorry place. ⓐ Str Vadul Moldovei 4 ⓣ 021 269 06 00 ⓦ www.zoobucuresti.ro ⓛ 10.00–17.00 daily ⓘ Admission charge

Insula Copiilor (Children's Island) A large children's playground with everything from inflatables to adventure trails, set on an island in the middle of Herăstrău Park. You can get to it by taxi or, more fun, by boat. ⓐ Parcul Herăstrău ⓣ 0721 223 272 ⓦ www.insulacopiilor.ro ⓛ 10.00–21.00 daily ⓘ Admission charge

Kids' Planet A large indoor playground where parents can enjoy a coffee. There's another outlet in City Mall. ⓐ Piaţa Alba Iuliu 2 ⓣ 021 326 60 46 ⓦ www.kidsplanet.ro ⓛ 14.00–22.00 Mon–Fri, 10.00–22.00 Sat, Sun & holidays ⓘ Admission charge

COMMUNICATIONS

Internet

Most good hotels provide free internet access and there are various Wi-Fi hotspots in the city. Mobile internet is available through the major mobile phone operators. Public internet cafés are a dying breed; you will still find the odd one though.

Phone

There are few public telephones in Bucharest, and all of them require a Romtelecom phone card. These can be bought from post offices or from most news-stands and kiosks, and cost 10–20 lei. Look out for the sign saying 'Avem cartele Romtelecom' ('We have Romtelecom phonecards').

All mobile operators cover the entire city and Bucharest is fully Blackberry-friendly. Check with your home network, however, regarding the cost of calls and messages, as they are usually very high. If you're staying for longer than a couple of weeks it is probably worth buying a local pay-as-you-go sim; it's quite easy to get your mobile unlocked for the purpose.

Post

The Central Post Office is at ⓐ Str Matei Millo 1 ⓣ 021 315 64 48 ⓦ www.posta-romana.ro ⓛ 07.30–13.00, 13.00–20.00 daily. Sending post is relatively cheap, but often slow.

TELEPHONING ROMANIA

To phone Bucharest from abroad, dial your international access code (usually 00), Romania's country code (40), followed by the Bucharest area code minus the initial 0 (21 or 31), and the local seven-digit number.

TELEPHONING WITHIN ROMANIA

For local calls just dial the seven-digit number. If calling Bucharest from elsewhere in Romania (or from a mobile) use the city code (021 or 031) too. Mobile phone numbers all have a four-digit prefix beginning with 07.

TELEPHONING ABROAD

Dial the international access code (00), followed by your country code, area code without the initial zero, and the number itself.

Country codes:
Australia 61
Canada 1
France 33
Germany 49
Ireland 353
New Zealand 64
South Africa 27
UK 44
USA 1

Directory enquiries 118 932

ELECTRICITY

The electricity supply is standard continental European 220 V, 50 Hz, which means that European appliances will work without a problem. Plugs are also standard European.

TRAVELLERS WITH DISABILITIES

Bucharest is not at all ready to receive disabled travellers. Its cracked, uneven pavements are a major hurdle, while public transport is completely inaccessible. Most public places are not yet adapted to handle wheelchairs, though EU legislation means that they should be in the mid-term future. Toilets for the disabled are rare. The more expensive hotels will be your best bet for accommodation.

TOURIST INFORMATION

Bucharest now finally boasts a tourist information centre in the University metro underpass (🅦 www.pmb.ro 🕘 09.00–18.00 Sun–Fri, 10.00–13.00 Sat). There's also a kiosk at Gara de Nord. Hotel staff can also give travel tips. The locally produced city guide *Bucharest In Your Pocket* (🅦 www.inyourpocket.com/romania/bucharest) is an indispensable resource. The following websites are also helpful: 🅦 www.psst.ro 🅦 www.romania.org 🅦 www.visitromania.com

BACKGROUND READING

Romania by Lucian Boia
Balkan Trilogy by Olivia Manning

Emergencies

EMERGENCY NUMBERS
Police ☎ 112 or 955
Fire ☎ 112 or 981
Ambulance ☎ 112 or 961

MEDICAL SERVICES
The main Accident and Emergency hospital for Bucharest is
Spitalul de Urgenţe (✉ Calea Floreasca 8, next to Dinamo Stadium
☎ 021 599 23 00 ⊕ www.urgentafloreasca.ro), where some staff
speak English. Emergency treatment is free for EU citizens with
a valid European Health Insurance Card (see Travel insurance
box, page 130) but you will be expected to pay for any drugs.
Some medical staff – though by no means all – may expect a tip.
Though the facilities may look somewhat rudimentary, the
standard of care is generally good. At the higher end of the

EMERGENCY PHRASES

Fire!	**Help!**	**Stop!**
Foc!	Ajutor!	Stop!
Fohc!	*Ajootor!*	*Stop!*

Call a doctor/the police/an ambulance!
Chemaţi doctorul/poliţia/salvarea!
Kematz doctorool/poleetzya/salvareya!

market are private medical clinics, such as **Medicover** (ⓐ Calea Plevnei 96 ☎ 021 310 44 10 ⓦ www.medicover.com ⓛ 08.00–20.30 Mon–Fri, 08.00–14.00 Sat) or **Euroclinic** (ⓐ Calea Floreasca 14 ☎ 021 200 68 00), which is open 24 hours.

Dental clinics include **BB Clinic** (ⓐ Calea Dorobanților 208 ☎ 021 320 01 51, emergencies 0728 38 73 73) and **Dent-A-America** (ⓐ Str Varsovia 4 ☎ 021 230 26 08 ⓦ www.dent-a-americainc.ro ⓛ 08.00–19.00 Mon–Fri, 08.00–12.00 Sat).

Pharmacies open 24 hours include **HelpNet** (ⓐ B-dul Unirii 24 ☎ 021 335 74 25) and **Sensiblu** (ⓐ Str Radu Beller 6 ☎ 021 233 89 61 ⓦ www.sensiblu.com).

POLICE

Inspectoratul General al Poliției ⓐ Șos Ștefan cel Mare 13–15 ☎ 021 208 25 25 ⓦ www.politiaromana.ro

EMBASSIES & CONSULATES

Australia ⓐ Str Titu Maiorescu 34E, Villa 7, Pipera-Voluntari ☎ 021 319 0229 ⓔ austral.consulat@gmail.com

Canada ⓐ Str Tuberozelor 1–3 ☎ 021 307 5000 ⓦ www.canadainternational.gc.ca

Ireland ⓐ Str Buzesti 50–52 ☎ 021 301 2131 ⓦ www.embassyofireland.ro

UK ⓐ Str Jules Michelet 24 ☎ 021 201 72 00 ⓦ www.ukinromania.fco.gov.uk

USA ⓐ Str Tudor Arghezi 7–9 ☎ 021 200 33 00 ⓦ www.romania.usembassy.gov

ACKNOWLEDGEMENTS

The publishers would like to thank the following individuals and organisations for supplying their copyright photographs for this book: Dreamstime, pages 5 (Imaengine), 17 (Viorel Dudau), 19 (Caranica Nicolae), 33 (Dobre Alexandru), 40–41 (Ciprian.d), 45 (Tudor Stanica), 109 (Ucebistu), 117 (Emi Cristea), 118 (Andreea Dobrescu), 120 (Lucertolone); Mediafax Foto, pages 101 & 115; Matt Musselman, pages 22–3; Romanian National Tourist Office, page 21; Vasile Szakacs, pages 26, 47, 81, 84, 94 & 127; Sorin Toma/Mediafax Foto, pages 106–7; World Pictures, pages 7, 49, 57 & 125; Craig Turp, all others.

Project editor: Ed Robinson
Layout: Trevor Double
Proofreaders: Rachel Norridge & Lucilla Watson

Send your thoughts to
books@thomascook.com

- Found a great bar, club, shop or must-see sight that we don't feature?
- Like to tip us off about any information that needs a little updating?
- Want to tell us what you love about this handy little guidebook and more importantly how we can make it even handier?

Then here's your chance to tell all! Send us ideas, discoveries and recommendations today and then look out for your valuable input in the next edition of this title.

Email the above address (stating the title) or write to:
pocket guides Series Editor, Thomas Cook Publishing, PO Box 227, Coningsby Road, Peterborough PE3 8SB, UK.

WHAT'S IN YOUR GUIDEBOOK?

Independent authors Impartial up-to-date information from our travel experts who meticulously source local knowledge.

Experience Thomas Cook's 165 years in the travel industry and guidebook publishing enriches every word with expertise you can trust.

Travel know-how Thomas Cook has thousands of staff working around the globe, all living and breathing travel.

Editors Travel-publishing professionals, pulling everything together to craft a perfect blend of words, pictures, maps and design.

You, the traveller We deliver a practical, no-nonsense approach to information, geared to how you really use it.

ABOUT THE AUTHOR

Craig Turp studied Romanian literature at university, and in 1996 went to live in the country for a year; he never came back. Now married with two young children, he is based in Bucharest, where he is the Publisher and Editor of *Bucharest In Your Pocket*, a locally produced guide to the Romanian capital that's published every two months.

Useful phrases

English	Romanian	Approx pronunciation

	BASICS	
Yes	Da	*Dah*
No	Nu	*Noo*
Please	Vă rog	*Vah rohg*
Thank you	Mulţumesc	*Mooltzoomesc*
Hello	Bună ziua	*Boonah zeeooa*
Goodbye	La revedere	*La revedereh*
Excuse me	Scuzaţi-mă	*Scoozatz-mah*
Sorry	Pardon	*Pardon*
That's okay	E în regulă	*Eh an rehgoolah*
I don't understand	Nu înţeleg	*Noo untzehleg*
Do you speak English?	Vorbiţi englezeşte?	*Vorbeetz englezeshteh?*
Good morning	Bună dimineaţa	*Boonah deemeeneyatzah*
Good afternoon	Bună ziua	*Boonah zeeooa*
Good evening	Bună seara	*Boonah sara*
Goodnight	Noapte bună	*Nwapteh boonah*
My name is ...	Mă numesc ...	*Mah noomesc ...*

	NUMBERS	
One	Unu/Una	*Oonoo/Oonaa*
Two	Doi	*Doy*
Three	Trei	*Tray*
Four	Patru	*Patroo*
Five	Cinci	*Chinc*
Six	Şase	*Saseh*
Seven	Şapte	*Shapteh*
Eight	Opt	*Opt*
Nine	Nouă	*Nowah*
Ten	Zece	*Zecheh*
Twenty	Douăzeci	*Dowahzech*
Fifty	Cincizeci	*Chinchzech*
One hundred	O sută	*Oh sooter*

	SIGNS & NOTICES	
Airport	Aeroport	*Aeroport*
Rail station	Gară	*Garah*
Platform	Peron	*Perohn*
Smoking/	Fumători/	*Foomahtoree/*
No smoking	Nefumători	*Nefoomahtoree*
Toilets	Toalete	*Twaleteh*
Ladies/Gentlemen	Femei/Bărbaţi	*Femay/Bahrbatz*
Metro	Metro	*Met-roh*